INTRODUCTION

*W*e all take photographs to capture the special times of our lives, but too often the pictures are stored away in boxes or drawers and are seldom looked at again. Your photos represent the history of your family for future generations and are worth taking the time to give them the attention they deserve. It's time to get them organized. The sooner the better.

The first thing to do is to make sure your photos are in a safe environment. Your photos can be damaged by extreme temperatures, humidity, dust, sunlight, "magnetic" albums, and contact with materials containing high acidity. Place them where they will be safe and begin organizing them as soon as possible.

Scrapbooking is all about organizing your photos and displaying them in albums. Journaling is telling the stories behind the pictures, which is a very important part of preserving your family history. You are creating albums filled with your family photos for you to enjoy now and to pass on to future generations. Someday people who never knew you will be looking at your albums. Create pages that represent you and the times of your life. Remember that the photos of your ordinary daily life are just as important as the special events.

The fun of scrapbooking is how you display the photos in your albums. Use the ideas in this book to inspire your creativity. There are many good ideas to choose from, but it will be your own personal photos that will guide you in creating pages that are totally unique. You will find that you will spend lots of time on some pages and do others quite quickly. You probably won't put all of your pictures in albums. You may want to pick out just the best ones and keep the others in files. However you decide you want to scrapbook, begin right away. Your family history is depending on you.

Julie

The following manufacturers' products and publishers' materials have been used to create the sample album pages in this book.

Accu-Cut Shape and Letter Cutting Systems®

American Traditional Stencils™

Creating Keepsakes™ Scrapbook Magazine

Delta Technical Coatings, Inc.
    Cherished Memories™ Stencils
    Cherished Memories ™ Acid-Free Paper
      Paint
    Ceramcoat® and Gleams™

EK Success Ltd.
    Border Buddy™
    ZIG® Memory System® Markers
    Inkworx® Air Art Gun
    Stickopotamus® Stickers

Fiskars® Inc.
    Paper Edgers, Corner Edgers, Circle Cutter, Personal Trimmer, Swivel Knife, Rotary Cutter, Cardstock, Photo Corners, Micro-Tip Scissors, Cutting Mat, Acrylic Ruler, Glue Pen
    McCall's Remember the Years™ Papers

Hot Off The Press, Inc.
    Paper Pizazz™
    Punch-Outs™

Krause Publications
    Great American Crafts Magazine
    Memory Magic Magazine

Memory Makers Magazine

Sticker Planet™
    Mrs. Grossman's™ Paper Company
    The Gifted Line® Stickers
    Sandylion Sticker Designs™

Xyron™ Adhesive Application & Laminating System

Table of Contents

21

28

32

46

More than Memories II

than

Beyond the Basics

Edited by

Julie Stephani

Copyright © 1999 by Krause Publications
All Rights Reserved

Published by

krause publications

700 East State Street, Iola, WI 54990-0001
Telephone (715) 445-2214
www.krause.com

Please call or write for our free catalog of publications. Our toll-free
number to place an order or obtain a free catalog is (800) 258-0929 or
please use our regular business telephone (715) 445-2214 for editorial
comment and further information.

Library of Congress Catalog Card Number: 98-85815

ISBN 0-87341-739-9

Manufactured in the United States of America

The content of this book is based on the
More Than Memories television show produced
by David Larson Productions.

67

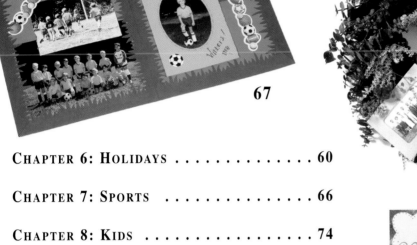

118

60

114

73

REVIEW & TECHNIQUES
GETTING STARTED

1. ORGANIZE PHOTOS AND NEGATIVES

Gather everything in one place where you can work undisturbed until you have time to sort through it all. Separate your photos into groupings and then work with one smaller group at a time. It's a good idea to place photos in chronological order by years. You may also use events to help you in grouping your pictures. For example, pictures in one group may be ones taken before you moved to a different town or pictures before someone was married or graduated from school.

Once you have pictures organized, store them in photo-safe containers. It will take time to get all of your photos into albums. You may only choose the very best photos for your albums and keep the others in files. Whatever you decide to do, it's important to label photos as soon as possible so people and events are identified.

2. PURCHASE SCRAPBOOK SUPPLIES

Start with the basics. You will need an **album with pages** included, or purchase paper and protective plastic sheets. For tools you need a **scissors, pencil, permanent pen, ruler, and an adhesive**. Make sure all of your materials are acid-free and photo safe. There are many more supplies to help you create beautiful pages such as decorative-edged scissors, a paper crimper, stencils and templates, paper paints, specialty markers, stamps, punches, die-cut shapes, and stickers. Half the fun of scrapbooking is using all of the creative materials available.

3. CHOOSE A THEME OR SUBJECT

Perhaps the easiest place to start is with a family album that begins with your most recent photos. It won't be overwhelming to keep current if you place photos in your albums right after they have been developed.

You may want to choose a theme album such as Christmas, or do an album commemorating an event such as a vacation, wedding, etc.

Gather your pictures together, and you are ready to be creative!

4. CROP AND MAT PHOTOS

Cropping a photo simply means that you cut away the unimportant or distracting background. Only crop when necessary to improve the focus on the subject. Do not cut any photo that can't be replaced. You can crop a photo using a ruler and scissors, a paper trimmer, or use a template to cut a photo in a special shape.

To mat a photo, place it on paper and cut a border around the photo. Choose colors of paper that will enhance the photos. Mats can be cut with straight or decorative-edged scissors for a variety of effects. Varying the width of the mats will also give you all kinds of creative possibilities.

5. LAY OUT PAGES

One of the most creative aspects of scrapbooking is arranging your photos and journaling on a page or pages. You want your pages to be attractive and organized so someone looking through your album can easily understand what is happening in the pictures on your pages. See more about layouts on page 10.

6. JOURNAL ON PAGES

Tell the story behind the photos in your album. Answer the questions Who? What? When? Where? Why? Give additional details to make the information more interesting. See more about journaling on page 12.

7. PRESERVE PAGES

Protect pages in plastic photo-safe plastic sheets. Collect pages in an album. Albums come in many sizes, but the most popular sizes that are readily available are 8½" x 11" and 12" x 12".

THREE-RING BINDER

- Rings open easily for adding or re-arranging pages.
- Protective sheets have three holes made to fit the rings.
- Plain or decorative papers can be inserted into protective sheets.
- "D"-shaped rings will allow pages to lie flat.

SPIRAL-BOUND ALBUM

- Set number of pages, sometimes with protective sheets.
- Will lie flat when open.
- Good quality covers in a variety of colors and patterns.

POST-BOUND ALBUM

- Bound with screws which can be taken apart.
- Extension posts can increase the depth of the album.
- High-quality cover.

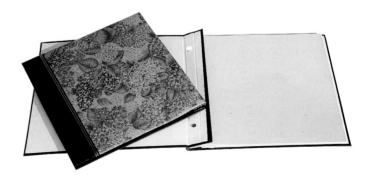

LAYOUTS: HOW TO DESIGN GREAT PAGES

A great scrapbook page . . .

Makes you smile

Evokes memories

Is attractive

Is readable and easy to understand

CHOOSING & CROPPING PHOTOS

Select several pictures with a common theme. After making the initial selection, review the photos a second time, eliminating any that are repetitious or just not good enough. From those, choose one or two to be the focal point of your page or pages. These will be the most eye-catching elements on the page.

Depending on your preference, make color photocopies or work with the original photos. Crop and shape the photos. Trim off any margins, distracting backgrounds, or blank spaces. Let the photo guide your cutting and shaping and keep it simple. Vary the shapes - combine ovals with rectangles and squares with circles for more eye appeal. You can cut photos in a variety of sizes and shapes using templates.

If you cut a silhouette (completely eliminating the background around the subject), when it comes time to mount it on the page, be sure to give it a base so it doesn't look like it's floating on the page. Be careful when cutting out silhouettes, leaving a very small amount of the background around the edge.

BACKGROUND

Select a background paper that will complement all of the photos, staying true to the theme and the colors represented in the photos. If the colors in your photos vary a lot, use the focus photo to determine the background. Use color to tie two pages together, including at least some of the same color on both pages. Color and texture add interest but shouldn't overwhelm or detract from the photos, which are the most important part of the page. If you use a busy patterned paper for the background, use contrasting solid colors for mats to pop the photos out of the page. You will find many examples in Chapters 2 through 14.

MATTING PHOTOS

Adding mats behind photos will introduce different shapes, colors, and textures to a page. You can make as many layers of mats as you like. Make sure the colors coordinate with the photos and all of the other mats as well as the background paper. Again, let the photo guide you in choosing shapes and colors for the mats. Many times the theme of the photo can be reinforced with the matting.

OTHER MEMORABILIA

Depending on the theme, you may have other pieces of memorabilia to include on the pages as well. Select the most meaningful items such as artwork, ticket stubs, menus, etc. For items that are too bulky or large to mount on the page, consider making pockets or envelopes to store them in. (See pages 14 and 15.)

EMBELLISHMENTS

Adding details to pages is fun, but it's also where you can go too far. Remember that the photos are the main attraction, so use stickers, die-cuts, cut-outs, etc. sparingly - only when they enhance the photos. Study the photos to find an element you could accent with an embellishment. A birthday party suggests wrapped presents, candles, birthday cake . . . you get the idea. If you notice that the page seems out of balance, you can correct it by adding an embellishment. Borders are another great way to tie elements together, particularly on two pages.

LAYOUTS

There is really no right or wrong way to arrange items on your pages, but there are guidelines to help you create visually appealing pages every time. Start by placing two blank pages side by side and begin playing with arrangements. Your pages should have a main focus and there should be a natural flow for your eyes to follow as you look at the pages. Vary the size of photos and mats and try different angles. If you are doing a two-page layout, make sure they complement each other.

Balance the "weight" of the items on each side of the center of two pages. Visually complex elements carry more weight than simple ones. Large items weigh more than small. This doesn't mean the page has to be symmetrical (the same on the left as it is on the right), although it can be. Asymmetrical (different on the left and right) pages can be balanced by offsetting one large photo with two smaller ones. Or use one brightly colored or textured mat to offset two plainer ones. Experiment with placing elements before gluing them down. You'll be able to tell if a page is balanced by how it strikes your eye - it's almost intuitive.

Try varying the angle of the photos on the page for visual interest and overlap photos often. Let photos "bleed" off the page by positioning them over the edge and trimming off the photo even with the edge of the page.

Remember to leave room for journaling - a very important part of the page. Journaling is another element that can be used to balance a page.

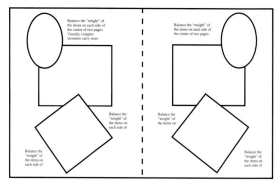

Symmetrical

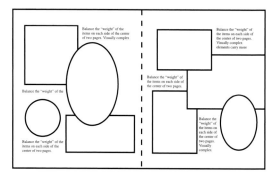

Asymmetrical

JOURNALING

When you are creating your memory albums, think about the people who will be thumbing through your wonderful photo displays in 100 years. Pictures can tell a story of their own, but if pictures have no journaling, the details are left completely to guesswork. With incomplete information, the story can become distorted over time. It's very important to include the accurate facts as well as your memories, thoughts, and feelings in your memory albums. You may be the only person in your family who takes the time to write these things down.

What a shame it would be if these stories were lost forever, leaving your children's children wondering about their roots.

The reason we use archival albums, acid-free paper, and fade-resistant ink is because we want our albums to last over time. What kinds of questions do you think future generations will have when looking at your pictures? What questions do you have when you look at old photos of past generations that have no journaling? We need to make sure that our albums are understood by including the names, dates, places, and stories behind the photos.

So where do you start? Don't be overwhelmed! The most important questions you can answer in your memory books are the simple questions "Who? What? When? Where?" If you can go further into the story, include the answers to "Why?" and "How?" To go one step further, hold the photo in front of you and ask yourself what sounds, sights, smells, textures, and feelings would describe the photo to someone else. These details will make the story more interesting. There are stories inside of each of us that no one will ever know unless we take the time to write them down.

If you don't like the idea of writing everything down, use your computer or a typewriter. If that still doesn't appeal to you, then use a tape recorder. Someone else can type or write the words for you later. The most important thing is that you do get the photos documented. If there are stories in your family that someone else knows better than you do, or if there are details that you do not know at all, use a tape recorder to interview your fact-knowing, story-telling relatives. Be sure to write down the information as soon as possible after the interview. The tape itself will be a cherished piece of memorabilia that can never be replaced. Imagine how wonderful it would be if you had a tape of your great-great-grandmother telling about the family and world news of her day.

Many people dislike their own handwriting, which keeps them from writing in their albums. Keep in mind that your own writing is also a piece of history, which will be cherished by the people who come after you. Imagine for a moment if you were handed ten sheets of paper with the exact same words written by different people. If your mother was one of the writers, would you be able to recognize her writing? Your handwriting is a part of you that can't be duplicated by anyone, so include it in your albums.

YOUR OWN HANDWRITING IS A PIECE OF HISTORY

Everyone takes photos of the big moments in life - graduations, weddings, the births of children, etc. These are important moments that deserve a special place in your scrapbooks. Be sure to include who was there, what happened, and where it all took place. It would be even better if you also included your memories of the event as well as those of other people who may have been there.

Some of the things that are the most fun to read about are the everyday things. Write about what a typical day in your life is like. Include pictures of the people you associate with, the places you go, and where you work. Write about the places you love to visit. Take pictures of and write about your children's schools, their friends, the places they play, their bedrooms. Take pictures of and write about your family's favorite foods, clothing styles, kinds of music they listen to, games they play, and your family traditions.

There are so many ways to document the moments of your life - just be sure to do it

When journaling, answer these questions. Who? What? When? Where? Why? and How?

some way. The small moments are what make the big moments what they are, so be sure to write about the things that you take for granted every day. Not only will you have a great time reading through what you wrote, but the people around you will love to read it, too. This is the gift that you are giving to future generations. These people will know all about you, your family, and your time of life. Make it the most interesting, inspiring, and educational book they have ever looked through!

Beautiful scrapbooks are becoming a wonderful part of this generation. In 100 years, there will be incredible heirloom books in so many families that have been passed through many different hands. Each memory book will be unique. Begin scrapbooking now and leave a family legacy for the future.

"Journaling" by Melody Ross, Chatterbox

POCKETS & ENVELOPES

Two of the easiest ways to include extensive journaling in your albums are by making envelopes or pockets. They will allow room for pages of typed or handwritten journaling and can be coordinated to fit right into the theme of any page. They can also be used to store memorabilia and other special items like recipes.

POCKETS

You can use just about any shape to create a pocket. It can look like an ordinary pocket or it can be an object like an apple. It just needs to be big enough to hold whatever you want to put in it. All you have to do is glue three sides of the pocket on the

page and leave the top open for inserting something. That's simple enough!

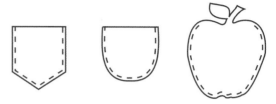

glue along dash lines

ENVELOPES

The easiest way to make an envelope is to find one the size you need and use it as a pattern. Just open up the envelope along the glued lines and trace around it. You can use patterned or plain paper for your envelope to match any theme. Cut the flap with paper edgers for a decorative touch.

To make your own envelope, decide what size you need and follow the simple drawings below.

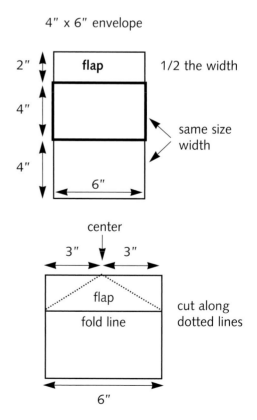

4" x 6" envelope

POCKET PAGES

Designs by Julie Stephani for Krause Publications

SUPPLIES

- Paper Pizazz: School Prints, Cutouts (School Days, Teen Years)
- ZIG MS Markers: Black Writer, White Opaque Writer
- Acid-free glue or Xyron Adhesive Cartridge

INSTRUCTIONS

Look at the fun kids can have making school pages that include pockets and envelopes to hold all kinds of fun memorabilia, notes, schedules, and secrets! Papers come with all kinds of school themes to choose from. Add die-cuts, punch-outs, cutouts and stickers to put colorful accents on the pages. Here are five fun pages to get you started. All you have to do is add the photos!

PHOTO TINTING

If you have admired the black and white photos that have been color tinted, you can color your own photos in the same way. There are a number of supplies to choose from and many of them can be purchased in kits that will include everything you need to get started.

BASIC TOOLS

- For photo oil paints: cotton swabs and balls, paper plate
- For water-based paints: #00 liner and #04 round paintbrushes
- Black & white photographs with matte finish

TINTING PRODUCTS

PHOTO OIL PAINTS*: Must be used on original matte-finished photographs. Glossy photos can be used if coated with matte-spray sealer. Use cotton swab to apply. Will take 3-5 days to dry completely. Can be purchased in kits.

PHOTO OIL PENCILS*: Can be used on photocopies. Come in limited colors. Need no drying time.

Spot Pen*: Markers formulated especially for photographs. Work on both glossy and matte surfaces. Come in 24 colors. Mistakes are easily wiped off. Drying time is 2-3 hours.

SoftTints*: Water-based gel paints. For added translucency, mix with blending medium. Work on color photocopies. Use paintbrush to apply. Mistakes can be

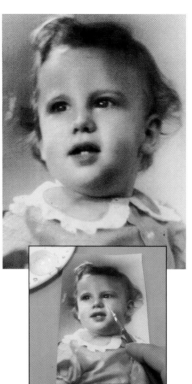

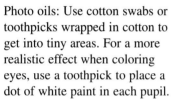

Photo oils: Use cotton swabs or toothpicks wrapped in cotton to get into tiny areas. For a more realistic effect when coloring eyes, use a toothpick to place a dot of white paint in each pupil.

Delta SoftTints were used on this color copy. To get natural lip and cheek colors, white was mixed with red. Hint: If you aren't coloring flesh tones, don't color the teeth or the whites of the eyes - they'll appear unnatural.

Pencils are great for small photos and tiny details such as lips or eyes. Soften the photo surface with pre-treatment solution if you are using oil pencils alone. Using oil pencils over photo oils does not require pre-treatment.

cleaned off with water. Drying time is 1-2 days.

COLORED LEAD PENCILS*: Choose soft leads. Can be used on color copies. Need no drying time.

PAINT MARKERS*: Give brilliant, opaque colors. Can be used on color copies. Need no drying time.

OIL-BASED PASTELS: Work in much the same way as oil paints. Can be a challenge to blend. Will work on color copies.

* The following companies are manufacturers of tinting products: John G. Marshall Mfg. Co. Inc. photo oils & pencils - Delta Technical Coatings, Inc. SoftTints & Color Float blending medium - ZIG MS by EK Success color markers.

BASIC RULES

Black and white photographs with a matte finish are essential for photo coloring. If you're developing new photos, ask your photo lab for matte paper. If you have an older photo with a gloss finish, you can either have a color photocopy made from the original or coat the entire photo with a matte finish. Any matte finish spray will work.

SHOOTING PHOTOS TO COLOR

If you are going to shoot your own black and white photos to handcolor, dress your subjects in light-colored clothing and try to keep busy little details out of the background. It's a good idea to have the entire print made 20%-30% lighter for optimum results. If the photo is too dark, the color will not show as well.

CAN I USE A COPY MACHINE?

If you are using handcoloring pens, gel paints, pencils, pastels, or paint markers (not photo oils or watercolors), a color photocopy of the original will work. (Use a color photocopier to get all the subtle shades of the black and white photo. Be sure to copy onto acid-free paper.) Like regular photos, lighter copies will work better than darker ones. Set the copier to print one or two stops lighter than normal.

WHAT ABOUT COLOR PHOTOS?

If you have a favorite color photograph that you'd like to handcolor, you can! Black and white prints can be made from color negatives (be sure to ask for matte paper.)

Reprinted from
How To Do Photo Tinting If You Think You Can't
published by Hot Off The Press.

PHOTO TRANSFERS

Photos are not just for albums. They can be transferred to fabric to create beautiful heirloom quilts, pillows, wall hangings, etc. You will need color copies of your photos.

BASIC SUPPLIES

- ❧ Access to a color laser copier
- ❧ Photo transfer paper
- ❧ Scotch tape
- ❧ Iron
- ❧ Scissors
- ❧ Glue
- ❧ Firm ironing surface, not padded
- ❧ Fusible webbing

GETTING STARTED

❶ Choose clear, bright photos to transfer. With copiers, photos can be enlarged or reduced to just about any size. To avoid wasting the transfer paper, arrange and tape the pictures on an 8½" x 11" sheet. Test the layout and color by making one copy on white paper, then follow manufacturer's directions on the photo transfer paper package. Hand feed the transfer paper through the copier with the coated side (unprinted) face up. The copy will be reversed when transferred unless the copy machine is set for mirror image. Cut each copied photo apart.

❷ Remove any lint or dust from the fabric and iron away wrinkles. Never prewash the fabric and do not use steam. Fabric suggested is 100% cotton but satin and moiré also give nice results. White fabric is preferred, but unbleached muslin can add warm tones or an antique look.

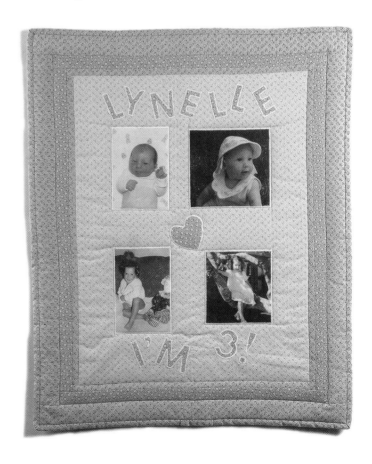

3 Place a lightweight towel over the ironing surface to protect it. For added weight, fill your iron with water (but remember, no steam). Preheat the iron on its highest setting, then warm the fabric. Lay the transfer paper face down on the fabric. Place the iron over the paper and press firmly over the entire surface. For large photos, iron in sections, 30 seconds at a time, then iron over the entire surface at least ten times to reheat the surface. After at least 30 seconds of heat, peel back a corner. If the transfer looks speckled, lay the corner back down and iron with even more pressure. If it looks good, quickly pull back the paper while it is still very hot.

4 To place a photo on an item that will not take the transfer directly, transfer the photo onto white fabric. Cut the photo from the fabric, leaving a white allowance on all edges. Follow the manufacturer's instructions to iron fusible web to the back of photo. Use either straight edge scissors or pinking shears to trim the edges of the photo. Peel off the web backing and use it to cover the front of the photo while ironing onto fabric. (This will prevent the photo from smudging.)

5 If you will be using fabric or dimensional paints on the transferred item, it is necessary to wash the item before painting it. If the transfer is directly on the item (white t-shirts for example), transfer the item and then wash the fabric before painting. If the item is colored and transfers must be attached with fusible web, wash the colored

item and transferred image together. Then paint as desired and iron the transfers on with the fusible web. For nonwearable items (such as pillows), transfer the photo onto unwashed fabric, then wash all materials.

Reprinted from Photo Transfer - What a Picture! *published by Hot Off The Press*

LAMINATING

One way to protect memorabilia that will deteriorate over time is to laminate it. Laminating is putting a plastic covering around an item, which creates a protective seal. It's the perfect way to protect newspaper clippings that will yellow and become brittle with age because of the high acid content of newsprint. Once clippings have been laminated, they are safe to put in your albums. Just think of all the things that you could preserve by laminating!

You can purchase laminating sheets, have items laminated by a professional, or use a laminating machine. Three models of machines* are available in different sizes, and each one can handle interchangeable cartridges that allow you to: 1) laminate both sides, 2) apply adhesive backing on

one side, or 3) laminate on one side and apply adhesive to the other side

The machines work without electricity or batteries. You simply place an item on the tray, turn the handle, and use the built-in cutter to cut the item loose. Laminating machines can be purchased, used at a scrapbook or craft store, or rented from a store for overnight use.

MAKING STICKERS

The same machines that are used for laminating can also be used to make stickers. You can make stickers from virtually anything that will fit through the rollers by using the cartridge that applies adhesive to one side of an item.

When the items have been run through the machine, they will be stuck to a backing. Then application is as simple as peel-and-stick. The glue has a set-up time, so you can reposition an item until it is placed exactly right.

* Xyron laminating machines are available in three models: the 850, the 2500, and the Pro 1250.

STENCILING

Stencils can be used on wood, fabric, paper, and any other paintable surface.

PREPARING TO STENCIL

Position the stencil as desired and tape it in place with masking tape. (Reduce the tackiness of the tape by sticking it on your clothing a few times.) You may also place a tape border around the edges of the stencil to prevent paint from being accidentally applied to the surface you're stenciling.

Always practice on paper first to perfect your color combinations and techniques.

STENCILING WITH ACRYLICS

❶ Squeeze a small amount of paint on the palette (paper and foam plates work well).

❷ Dip the brush into the paint and briskly swirl it on a paper towel or piece of scrap paper to remove excess paint and distribute the paint evenly throughout the bristles. The brush should feel dry to the touch. This *dry brush* is critical for smooth, crisp, stenciled images. To keep colors clean, rinse the brush with water between colors and dry thoroughly with a towel.

STENCILING WITH OIL STICKS OR CREAMS

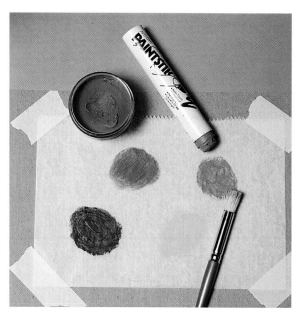

❶ Remove the protective skin from oil paints with a paper towel before using.

❷ When working with paint pots, dip the brush into the jar, then rub onto the palette. (Non-porous surfaces such as wax paper or foam plate works well for oils.) Rub oil sticks on the palette, then tap the brush into the smear.

❸ Use a separate brush for each color. Clean the brushes with soap and water when finished or use a brush cleaner.

STENCILING TECHNIQUES

The only real RULE in stenciling is to use very little paint. The following techniques show different ways of applying paint. Use one method or all of them. Here, a brush is being used for better coverage and shading control, but you may prefer a sponge or other applicator.

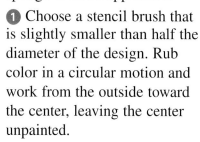

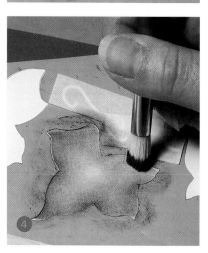

❶ Choose a stencil brush that is slightly smaller than half the diameter of the design. Rub color in a circular motion and work from the outside toward the center, leaving the center unpainted.

❷ Paint the entire design with a rubbing motion, working from the outside of the stencil in.

❸ Create a stippled effect by holding the brush upright and rapidly tapping the color onto the surface.

❹ Use multiple colors to achieve more natural shading. Begin with the lightest color (usually yellow) and add a darker tone, blending colors to create new hues (for example, red over yellow creates orange).

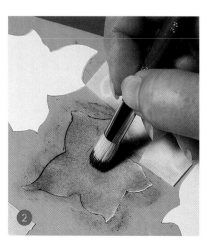

EMBOSSING

Add dimension to your paper by creating raised designs using stencils and a stylus tool. It will give your pages an elegant touch which is perfect for weddings, and other special occasions.

PRESSURE EMBOSSING

❶ Tape the stencil in place on your paper. Flip the paper over and place it on a light source (a light box or window).

❷ Use the larger end of an embossing stylus to trace the design. To help the stylus glide smoothly over the paper, rub your clean fingers over the paper to add moisture.

❸ Flip the paper back over. If you want to add color, tape the stencil on your paper and stencil as desired. When finished, carefully remove the stencil and tape.

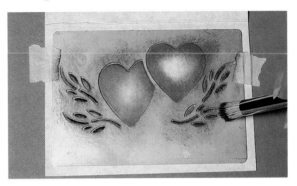

THERMAL EMBOSSING

❶ While ink/paint is wet, sprinkle with embossing powder and gently tap off excess.

❷ Hold the paper near a heat source (heat gun, steam iron, warming tray, or toaster) until the powder melts.

Note: Dark paper can also be embossed even though you can't see the stencil design using a light source. For this method, you will need two identical stencils. One stencil is placed on each side of the paper. The stencils must be exactly aligned. The top stencil is the embossing guide.

Stenciling and Embossing information courtesy of American Traditional Stencils.

DIMENSIONAL PAGES

Adding dimension to your scrapbook pages is easy with pop-ups, pop-arounds, and pop-outs. They may look complicated, but once you get the idea, you won't want to stop. The secret of the three techniques is in the folding. Practice with scraps of paper first. Once you see the mechanics of how each technique works, you'll be looking for all kinds of ways to use them on your pages.

POP-UPS

To make a pop-up, cut a basic pop-up base from heavyweight paper (65 lb. works well) using the pattern shown. Fold the basic shape in half. Fold the bottom edges upwards toward the outside. Glue the bottom edges on your scrapbook pages on either side of the center. Glue photographs, die-cut shapes, punch outs, etc. to "pop out" off the page when it is opened on the remainder of the shape above the fold line. There is a rule that you must keep in mind - the pop-up figure shouldn't be any taller than the length of the page from the bottom edge to the center fold of the pop-up base.

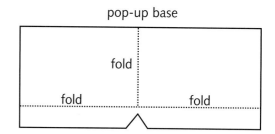

pop-up base

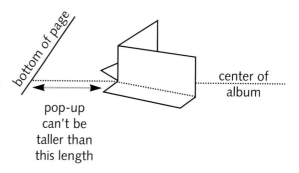

pop-up can't be taller than this length

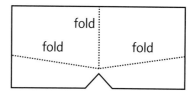

fold bottom edges at an angle to make pop-up lean back

pop-up

POP-OUTS

Cut the shape three, four, or as many times as you would like, having at least one outer edge overlapping so the shapes are connected (see illustration). You can also fold your paper accordion-style ahead of time and just cut one shape that will unfold into a chain. A paper-doll chain is a good example. You need to keep in mind that the pleat of the folds should be just slightly smaller than the design so the design will extend beyond the folds slightly. Don't cut where the design extends beyond the paper, and the designs will be connected when you unfold the paper.

POP-AROUNDS

Glue the end shapes of the chain on your scrapbook pages on either side of the fold. The simplest way to do this is to apply glue on the bottom shape. Place the shape firmly on the page on the right side of the fold. Don't unfold the chain. Apply glue on the shape that is now facing up, then close the second page on the folded shapes. Let the glue take hold. When you open the page, the chain will be glued to the left page and will automatically pull apart. The pink daisy flowers are a good example of a pop-out.

The pop-around is similar to the pop-out except the chain is cut in a circle and the bottom two designs are cut away. To make the shapes stand up from the pages, glue the end shapes on the right and left side of the fold. How much the shapes will stand up from the page depends on the distance

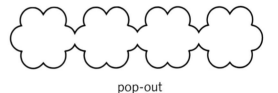

pop-out

between the glued shapes. For example, if you want your pop-around to be slightly raised from the page, the glued shapes will have the maximum space between them. To make the pop-around stand up more, glue the shapes closer together.

pop-around

HOME & FAMILY

NEW BEGINNINGS

Design by Toni Nelson for EK Success

SUPPLIES

- Paper Pizazz: Gold (Plain Brights)
- Border Buddy: #5 Camelot
- ZIG MS Markers: Fine & Chisel - Red, Apricot
  Calligraphy - Apricot
  Writer - Black

- Stickopotamus Stickers: Construction
- Acid-free glue or Xyron Adhesive Cartridge

INSTRUCTIONS

1. Draw border using template and red Chisel tip marker. Connect corners and create boxes with the straight edge from the grass cutout.
2. Mat photos on gold paper and glue on page.
3. Edge small rectangles with broad tip of Calligraphy

pen, then edge again with Chisel tip. Write day numbers on rectangles and glue on page.
4. Add sticker accents around boxes and photos. Doodle around stickers with black pen. Write title.

Design by Beth Reames for EK Success

MOM'S GARDEN GROWS

SUPPLIES

- Paper Pizazz: Pink, Lavender, Green (Plain Brights)
- White paper
- Border Buddy: #5 Camelot
- ZIG MS Markers: Fine & Chisel - Pink, Green
  Writers - Green, Baby Pink, Hyacinth, Violet, Pink, Yellow
  Calligraphy - Pink
  Scroll & Brush - Green
- Acid-free glue or Xyron Adhesive Cartridge

INSTRUCTIONS

1. Draw border around page with Aristocrat border and pink Chisel tip.
2. Add dots, flowers and squiggles along border. Place photos on page to determine placement of flowers. Draw flowers. Add leaves and doodles.
3. Mat photos on colored paper and glue on page.
4. Cut white rectangles for lettering. Edge rectangles with broad tip of Calligraphy pen. Write letters and glue rectangles on page.

OPEN DOOR

SUPPLIES

- ∞ American Traditional Stencils: GS-125 Screen Door, BL-477 Oval Cameo Frame, BL-90 Ivy Theme Pack, BL-676 Scroll
- ∞ 8" x 9" brown parchment album page
- ∞ 6" x 8½" off-white cardstock
- ∞ 5" x 6" white cardstock
- ∞ Fiskars: Seagull Paper Edgers
- ∞ Paints: gray, green, brown, yellow, red, blue
- ∞ 3/16" stencil brush
- ∞ Art knife
- ∞ Glitter (optional)
- ∞ Acid-free glue or Xyron Adhesive Cartridge

Design by Judy Barker for American Traditional Stencils

INSTRUCTIONS

Note: See Stenciling General Instructions on page 19.

1. Position oval stencil on off-white cardstock. Stencil green/gray ribbon oval and brown corner lines. With pencil, lightly trace around oval. Cut out center oval.

2. Trim paper borders with Seagull edgers. Drybrush brown along outside edge.

3. Stencil door in center of white cardstock. Make clapboards by drybrushing brown off straight edge of paper. Carefully move down 1/2" at a time from top of cardstock to doorstep. Drybrush brown under doorstep. Stencil a sprig of ivy on left side of doorstep and flower pot on right side. *Option: Glue glitter on screen door, lantern and flower pot.*

4. Use art knife to cut along three sides of door. Glue photo behind door opening Glue door piece behind oval opening.

5. Stencil scroll design on right and left side of album page. Drybrush brown around edge and in between the scroll.

6. Stencil ivy on a scrap of oval cardstock or on another album page. Cut out and glue on album page. Drybrush brown around each cluster.

GRANDPA'S 75TH BIRTHDAY

SUPPLIES

- ❧ Paper Pizazz: Cream, Green (Plain Pastels), Dark Green (Solid Muted)
- ❧ Black paper
- ❧ Fiskars: Paper Edgers - Victorian
  Corner Edgers - Regal, Nostalgia
  Personal Paper Trimmer
  McCall's Remember the Years™ 1900-1929 Paper
  Photo Corners
- ❧ ZIG MS Markers: Black Writer
- ❧ Watch clip art
- ❧ Ruler
- ❧ Acid-free glue or Xyron Adhesive Cartridge

Design by Fiskars, Inc.

INSTRUCTIONS

1. Mat photo on cream paper with photo corners, leaving 1" border at bottom for title.
2. Make folded corners as follows: Cut four 1" x 2" each pieces of light green, white and dark green paper. Score along fold lines. Cut one long edge of each piece with Victorian edgers. Layer one piece of each color and fold corners under. Slip corners on photo.
3. Glue cream paper on black paper, gluing at corners only. Cut 1/4" border. Mat black paper on green paper,

leaving 1¼" border at bottom for list of names. Trim four corners of green paper with Regal corner edgers.
4. For nameplate, type list of names on light green paper or write names by hand. Trim green paper with the paper trimmers. Trim four corners of nameplate with Nostalgia corner edgers. Embellish corners of nameplate with black Writer. Glue matted photo on patterned paper.
5. Add clip art.

Design by Julie Stephani for Krause Publications

LACE TRIMMED FRAME

SUPPLIES

- ❧ Any size frame
- ❧ 1"-wide ecru gathered lace with beaded edge
- ❧ 1/8"-wide ecru satin ribbon
- ❧ 1" ecru satin flower
- ❧ Acid-free glue or Xyron Adhesive Cartridge

INSTRUCTIONS

Turn any frame into a lovely Victorian frame by adding lace with ribbon accents. Glue lace around frame, overlapping ends where flower will be placed. Make a multi-

loop bow and glue over lace ends. Glue satin flower in center of bow. Glue ribbon ends along side of frame. Cut ribbon ends at a slant.

MOTHER GERTRUDE

SUPPLIES

- ❧ Paper Pizazz: Purple Flowers (Floral Papers), Ferns (Great Outdoors) Blue, Green (Solid Muted Colors), Pretty Alphabet Punch-Outs
- ❧ White paper
- ❧ Fiskars: Deckle Paper Edgers
- ❧ Oval template
- ❧ Acid-free glue or Xyron Adhesive Cartridge

INSTRUCTIONS

1. For border on left side of page, cut a 1¼"-wide strip from fern paper. Mat on blue paper, then on green paper trimmed with Deckle edgers. Glue a 1/4" green strip down center of strip. Glue punchout letters down center of strip. Glue strip on page.

2. Cut photo in an oval. Mat photo on blue paper, then fern paper, then green paper. Glue on page.

3. Type journaling on white paper. Cut into a rectangle. Mat on green, then blue paper. Glue rectangle on page.

Design by Becky Goughnour for Hot Off The Press

Gertrude White Russell
We celebrated Mom's 85th birthday this year.
(She was born December 12, 1912, or 12-12-12.)
Many family members and friends gathered to honor her.
She is much loved for her kind and gracious spirit.

PICNICS

SUPPLIES

- Paper Pizazz: Red, Yellow, Green (Plain Brights), Lavender (Plain Pastels)
- Red gingham paper
- White paper
- ZIG MS Markers: Writers - Red, Black
- Large and small circle punches
- Acid-free glue or Xyron Adhesive Cartridge

INSTRUCTIONS

1. Mat photos on green paper. Glue on page.
2. Cut white rectangles with rounded corners for journaling. Write journaling on rectangles and mat on colored paper. Glue on page.
3. Punch large circle flowers from purple and red paper. Cut small circle flower centers from yellow paper.
4. Glue flowers around largest photo. Add green leaves.
5. Draw larger flowers and cut from paper. Glue on page.

*Design by Becky Higgins for
Creating Keepsakes Magazine*

Design by Julie Stephani for Krause Publications

1. Cut corners of one large photo with Nostalgia corner edgers. Mat photo on yellow, then pink paper, cutting corners in same way. Save corners you cut off. Glue photo on page. Glue yellow cut-off corners on each corner, leaving a space.
2. Mat other large photo on yellow paper and cut with Bubbles edgers. Mat on turquoise paper and glue on

KATRINA

SUPPLIES

- Paper Pizazz: Yellow, Pink, Turquoise (Plain Brights), Geometric (Birthday)
- Fiskars: Paper Edgers - Bubbles, Scallop
  Corner Edgers - Blossom, Nostalgia
- ZIG MS Markers: Black Writer
- Accu-Cut Dies: Bunny, Small Hearts
- Circle template
- Acid-free glue or Xyron Adhesive Cartridge

INSTRUCTIONS

page. Glue pink cut-off corners on each corner.
3. Cut one photo in a circle and mat on turquoise paper. Cut with Scallop edgers. Mat on pink paper and cut with same edgers. Glue on page.
4. Cut a yellow rectangle for journaling. Cut with Bubbles corner edgers. Mat on turquoise paper and glue on page.
5. Arrange die-cuts on page. Write journaling on die-cuts and rectangle. Add small dot accents around paper edges.

FUNNY FARM

Design by Julie Stephani for Krause Publications

SUPPLIES

- Paper Pizazz: Flecked Tan (Solid Muted), Gold, Green (Plain Brights), Brown (Solid Jewel Tones)
- Fiskars: Paper Edgers - Scallop, Victorian, Pinking, Dragonback
  Corner Edgers - Nostalgia
- ZIG MS Markers: Black Writer, Brown Calligraphy
- Templates: oval, circle
- Acid-free glue or Xyron Adhesive Cartridge

INSTRUCTIONS

You need to do some creative cropping to get ten photos on just two pages! Silhouette some photos to eliminate excess background. Mat photos with narrow single or double mats, cutting straight edges and a variety of decorative edges. Use only three colors for mats to tie them together. To save space, photos overlap each other and even "bleed" off the pages. Add accents with the black marker. Draw the board-looking title using the brown Calligraphy marker.

THE NELSONS

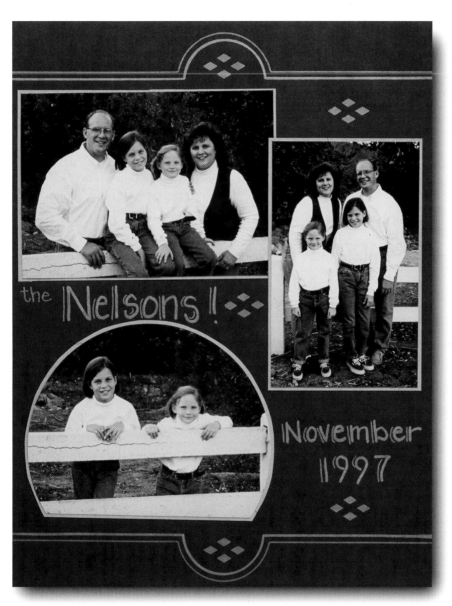

Design by Toni Nelson for EK Success

SUPPLIES

- Paper Pizazz: Brown (Solid Jewel Tones), Tan (Plain Pastels)
- Border Buddy 6: Romantic
- ZIG MS Markers: Opaque Writers - Extra Fine Copper, Fine Copper
- Acid-free glue or Xyron Adhesive Cartridge

INSTRUCTIONS

1. Draw borders across top and bottom of page with a cutout border and fine and extra-fine tip Writers. Add diamonds in centers.

2. Mat photos on tan paper and glue on page.

3. Draw random diamonds and journal using both Writer pens.

CHAPTER 3

HERITAGE

SILVERWARE AND MARRIAGE CERTIFICATE

SUPPLIES

- Paper Pizazz: Green (Solid Jewel Tones)
- Black cardstock
- ZIG MS Markers: Gold Extra-Fine Opaque Writer, Gold Fine & Chisel
- Fiskars: Colonial Paper Edgers
- Inkworx Air Art Gun
- Acid-free glue or Xyron Adhesive Cartridge

INSTRUCTIONS

Design by Carol Snyder for EK Success

Note: Dimensional silverware, bowl, and lace doily were laid face down on a color copy machine and copied. A black sheet of paper was held behind the doily.

1. For gold edge on green silverware background paper, cut a 2" x 11" strip of cardstock for a template. Trim edges with Colonial edgers. Lay template along one edge with decorative peaks facing edge of green paper, about 1/4" from edge. Draw a line along template with extra-fine gold marker. Repeat for other three sides. Color to edge of paper with fine gold marker.

2. For gold edge on green certificate background paper, lay template along one edge with decorative peaks facing edge of green paper, about 1/2" from edge. Using art gun and fine gold marker, spray a fine gold mist from decorative edge to paper edge. Repeat for other three sides. Add gold line with extra-fine gold marker and gold dots in peaks. Cut around color copy of lace and place on center of page.

3. Trim around photos with Colonial edgers and mat on black paper. Make a border around edge of mat with gold Chisel marker. Use extra-fine gold marker for accents. Add journaling.

17 June 1896

Laura A. Howe

Robert H. Trott

MARRIAGE CERTIFICATE

STATE OF UTAH.

COUNTY OF SALT LAKE

This Certifies that Robert H. Trott of Big Cottonwood in the State of Utah, and Laura A. Howe of Murray in the State of Utah, were by me joined together in **Holy Matrimony** according to the Ordinance of God and the Laws of the State of Utah, at Salt Lake City in said County, on the 17th day of June in the year of Our Lord One Thousand Eight Hundred and Ninety six

In the presence of

George Romney   John Cutder

W. D. Kier

Elder of the Church of Jesus Christ of Latter-day Saints.

BLACK & WHITE HERITAGE RIBBON CARD

SUPPLIES

- ❧ 38" black polka-dot 1"-wide grosgrain ribbon
- ❧ Black mounting board or cardstock
- ❧ Sticker borders
- ❧ Acid-free glue or Xyron Adhesive Cartridge

Design by Dee Gruenig for Xyron

INSTRUCTIONS

Note: There is a photo on both sides of each mounting board.

1. Make photocopies of even number of favorite old photographs, enlarging or reducing them to same size. Cut same number of pieces of black mounting board, 1" larger all around

2. Run photographs through the Xyron, using acid-free adhesive, then peel and stick one to center of each board piece.

3. Run half the boards through Xyron, using acid-free adhesive. Peel liner and lay them face down 1/2" apart (with adhesive exposed).

4. Lay ribbon down on center of each board, having 1/2" of ribbon between each board. Press on remaining boards, sandwiching ribbon.

5. Cut sticker borders to fit around photos as frames.

GRANDPA ABC

*Designs by Katie Knight
for Memory Makers Magazine*

SUPPLIES

- Paper Pizazz: Brown, 2 Blues (Solid Jewel Tones), Dots (Dots, Checks, Plaids, Stripes)
- Black paper
- Fiskars: Deckle Paper Edgers
- ZIG MS Markers: Black Writer
- Accu-Cut Dies: Letters
- Circle and oval templates
- Acid-free glue or Xyron Adhesive Cartridge

INSTRUCTIONS

When you are giving a special memory album, letters of the alphabet can carry a theme throughout the pages. Think of something special to say with each letter. You can also write a poem to fit the gift recipient and feature it on the first page. Use the letters in the person's name as the first letter of each line.

Be sure to do lots of journaling throughout the album!

AUNT FLORENCE

SUPPLIES

- Paper Pizzazz: Burgundy (Solid Jewel Tones), Tan, Pink (Plain Pastels)
- Fiskars: Swivel Knife
  Paper Edgers - Provincial, Sunflower, Scallop
  Corner Edgers - Nostalgia
  McCall's Remember the Years™ 1900-1929 Paper
- ZIG MS Markers: Black Writer
- Oval template
- Book clip art
- Acid-free glue or Xyron Adhesive Cartridge

Design by Fiskars, Inc.

INSTRUCTIONS

1. Glue photo on tan paper. Trim mat with Provincial edgers.
2. Continue matting photo with seven layers, varying colors from light to dark. Trim mats with different edgers. For a dramatic look, vary width of mats.
3. Position matted photo on background paper and lightly mark where matted photo overlaps graphic lady design. With swivel knife, cut around design, making sure not to cut beyond marked area.
4. Slide matted photo into slot and glue in place.
5. Cut tan rectangle for journaling and trim corners with Nostalgia corner edgers. Mat on burgundy and trim in same way. Print journaling. Glue on clip art.

Design by Fiskars, Inc.

UNCLE BOB

SUPPLIES

- Paper Pizzazz: Dark Green (Solid Jewel Tones), Cream, Tan, Green (Plain Pastels)
- Fiskars: 45mm Rotary Cutter with Squiggle & Straight blades
  Art Deco Corner Edgers
  5" Micro-Tip Scissors
  McCall's Remember the Years™ 1940-1949 Papers
- ZIG MS Markers: Black Writer
- Golf clubs clip art
- Acid-free glue or Xyron Adhesive Cartridge

INSTRUCTIONS

1. Punch template from center of Remember the Years paper and enlarge to fit photo. Trace it on 6½" x 8½" sheet of tan paper, leaving enough room for nameplate at bottom of page. Cut out shape.
2. Trim long edges with Squiggle rotary cutter and glue onto 7" x 8½" sheet of creme colored paper.
3. Create mat look for cutout by cutting around cutout area with Micro-Tip scissors, leaving 1/4" creme edge. Glue photo on mat. Glue mat on background paper.
4. Cut strip of light green paper 1" x 8½". Trim one long edge with Squiggle rotary cutter. Cut strip of dark green paper 1/2" x 8½". Trim both long edges with Squiggle rotary cutter.
5. Glue dark green strip along edge of light green strip. Glue both on right edge of light brown paper.
6. Cut one 1" x 8½" strip from light green and one from dark green. Trim long edges of both with Squiggle rotary cutter. Position and glue on left side of light brown paper.
7. Cut cream rectangle for journaling and trim corners with Art Deco corner edgers. Mat with light green, then dark green paper, cutting corners in same way.
8. Add clip art and journaling.

HISTORIC EVENTS

War News: Casablanca Conference Between Churchill and Roosevelt; Japanese Driven from Guadalcanal; Eisenhower Announces Italy's Unconditional Surrender Sept. 8; Italy Declares War on Germany; Russians Take Kiev; U.S. Forces Regain Islands in Pacific; Churchill, Stalin, and Roosevelt Hold Tehran Conference; Students Hans and Sophie Scholl Distribute Anti-Nazi Pamphlets in Munich and are Caught and Executed; Allied "Round-the-Clock" Bombing of Germany Begins.

1943

Penicillin Successfully Used in the Treatment of Chronic Diseases
Waksman and Schatz Discover Streptomycin
1500-Mile-Long "Big Inch" Oil Pipeline, From Texas to Pennsylvania Begins Operation
Charlie Chaplin Marries Oona O'Neill
President Roosevelt Freezes Wages, Salaries and Prices to Forestall Inflation
Infantile Paralysis Epidemic Kills Almost 1200 in U.S., Cripples Thousands More
Shoe Rationing Begins in U.S., Followed by Rationing of Meat, Cheese, Fats, and All Canned Foods
U.S. War Labor Board Orders Coal Mines to be Taken Over by the Government When ½ Million Miners Strike
Pay-as-you-go Income Tax System Instituted in U.S.
Jackson Pollock's First One-Man Show

"That's why Hitler surrendered"
Don Myers

Glenn Harold + Edna

Race Riots Break Out in Several Major U.S. Cities Whose Labor Population Has Been Bolstered by Influx of Southern Blacks
Martha Graham Dances in "Deaths and Entrances"
Deaths of: George Washington Carver, Stephen Vincent Benét, Rachmaninoff, and Max Von Schillings (German composer and conductor)

Charles Lynn Sherwberry

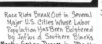
Jeannine Altman

"Casablanca" Wins Academy Award
"Oklahoma!" Reaches 2,248 Consecutive Performances in New York
Zoot Suit (with Reet Pleat) Becomes Popular Attire Among Hepcats in U.S.
Lindy Hop Yields to Jitterbugging in U.S.
Popular Songs: "Mairzy Doats", "Oh, What a Beautiful Mornin", "People Will Say We're In Love", "Comin' in on a Wing and a Prayer"

Jeannine and Skippy

SUPPLIES

- Paper Pizazz: Blue, Green, Brown (Solid Jewel Tones)
- White or ivory cardstock
- ZIG MS Markers: Writers - Black, Brown
- Stickers
- Acid-free glue or Xyron Adhesive Cartridge

Design by Anita Hickenbotham for Memory Makers Magazine

MANSFIELD NEWS-JOURNAL

VOL. 77, NO. 251 • PHONE LA 2-2511 MANSFIELD, OHIO, WEDNESDAY, FEBRUARY 21, 1962 SEVEN CENTS

Astronaut Relaxes After Voyage

Experts Quiz Glenn On Trip

Flight Hailed By Millions

1962

U.S. Military Council Established in S. Vietnam
Georges Pompidou Forms Government in France
Adolf Eichmann Hanged
U Thant Elected UN Secretary-General
Thalidomide Causes Children to be Born with Malformations
U.S. Spacemen Glenn, Carpenter and Schirra orbit separately
An Earthquake in Northwestern Iran Kills 10,000
Second Vatican Council Opens in Rome

John Glenn travels by space capsule, the Myers' get around in this family-size station wagon

Glenn Just The Start

'Couldn't Feel Better'
Glenn Taken To Island Hideaway

Khrushchev Wan To Pool Resource

Daily Chuckl

HAPPY BIRTHDAY

...Laurie Turns Five...

INSTRUCTIONS

To commemorate a special day, copy news clippings and other memorabilia and mount them on a page. Don't use original newsprint, as it will deteriorate quickly. Crop photos and mat them on colored paper. Write the title and journal historical information with different colored pens. Add sticker accents.

*Designs by Joanna Randolph Rott
for Krause Publications*

SUPPLIES

- 11" x 12¾" Walnut Hollow Farm frame
  (4½" x 6½" center opening)
- Delta: Black Ceramcoat acrylic paint
    Gold Gleams paint
    Top Coat Satin spray
    Decoupage medium
- Plasti-Kote: Classic Pearls Spray Paint -
  Black Basecoat, Touch of Gold Topcoat
- Fiskars: Scallop Paper Edgers

- 10 Woodsie 1½" squares
- 10 pairs of Velcro disks
- 1" brass ring
- 10 gold paper clips
- 9" x 12" black felt
- 40 black photo corners
- 1⅓ yard of 1/2"-wide gold braid
- Lightweight cardboard
- Acid-free glue

INSTRUCTIONS

Note: Let paint and finishes dry between coats. Photos can be laminated in place of covering with decoupage.

Large Frame

1. Spray three coats of black base coat over front and edges of frame. To mask off corners, cut eight A corner patterns from cardboard. Tape cardboard corners on corners of front and back of frame. Mask off frame corner edges with tape. Spray two coats of gold topcoat paint on entire frame. Dip end of paintbrush in gold paint and place dot on each corner. Spray with finishing spray.

2. Using finger, apply glue around outside rim of frame. Press braid around frame, beginning and ending at top center. Screw brass ring into top center of frame.

3. Cut strips of black felt with scallop scissors and glue around inside opening of frame. Glue photo on 5" x 7" piece of cardboard. Paint photo with several coats of decoupage. Apply glue on back of felt mat and press photo in place. Tape 10" x 12" cardboard backing on back of frame.

4. Journal (names, places, dates) on 5" x 7" piece of paper and glue on back of frame.

Small Mini Frames

5. Make ten photocopies, enlarging or reducing as needed to fit 1½" squares. Trace one Woodsie square on each photo and cut out. Glue four black photo corners on each photo. Paint each square black. When dry, glue one photo on each square. Place squares under heavy object for several hours. Paint squares with several coats of decoupage

6. Cut ten 1½" squares of black felt. Glue felt squares on back of wooden ones. Dip round toothpick in gold acrylic paint and place dot on each photo corner as shown. For hanger, glue paper clip on center back of each photo square, having 1/4" of paper clip show above photo frame.

7. Glue Velcro disks on center back of each square. Position frames on larger frame. Glue matching Velcro circles on larger frame. Press small photo frames on Velcro circles on large frame.

corner A
cut 8
cardboard

VINTAGE PHOTO PLANT POKE

SUPPLIES

- Delta: Black Ceramcoat acrylic paint Gold Gleams paint Decoupage medium
- 1 gold paper clip
- 1 Woodsie 1½" square
- Black felt
- 4 small black photo corners
- Round toothpick
- Pony bead
- 1/4 yard gold embroidery floss
- 8" length #18-gauge green covered wire
- Green florist tape
- Small sprig of ivy
- Acid-free glue

INSTRUCTIONS

1. Follow steps 5-7 above to make one mini frame. Tie several short lengths of gold floss on top of paper clip.

2. Wrap 7" length of covered wire with floral tape. Glue wire to back of photo frame, extending wire 1" above top of frame. Insert wire through pony bead. Bend wire and place end in bead. Glue sprig of ivy on back of frame.

VINTAGE PHOTO NECKLACE

SUPPLIES

- ❧ Delta: Black Ceramcoat acrylic paint
  Gold Gleams paint
  Decoupage medium
- ❧ 16 gold paper clips
- ❧ 16 Woodsie 1½" squares
- ❧ Black felt
- ❧ 64 small black photo corners
- ❧ Round toothpick
- ❧ 3 yards black leather cord
- ❧ 23 gold pony beads
- ❧ 32 gold jump rings
- ❧ Gem Tac glue

INSTRUCTIONS

1. Photocopy 16 vintage photos. Follow steps 5-7 on page 39 to make mini frames.

2. Fold leather cord in half. See figures below. Weave right end of cord through right hole on bead. Then weave left end of cord through left hole on bead. Add beads and continue weaving in this way. Space beads evenly to form 3/4" width loops as shown. Weave 21 beads.

3. Thread cord ends through one bead. Measure length of necklace so it will slip easily over your head and cut off excess at loop end.

4. Separate two gold rings and place them through paper clip on one photo frame. Slip both open rings through third loop (link) from either end of chain. Close ring by pressing ends together. Continue adding photo frames to leather chain until necklace is complete.

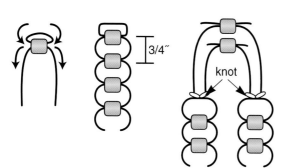

VINTAGE PHOTO PIN

SUPPLIES

- Delta: Black Ceramcoat acrylic paint
    Gold Gleams paint
    Decoupage medium
- 1 gold paper clip
- 1 Woodsie 1½" square
- Black felt
- 4 small black photo corners
- Round toothpick
- 1½ yards gold embroidery floss
- 10mm earring pad
- Acid-free glue

INSTRUCTIONS

1. Follow steps 5-7 on page 39 to make one mini frame.
2. Tie several short lengths gold floss in bow on top of paper clip. Glue earring pad on back of frame.

VINTAGE PHOTO TISSUE BOX

SUPPLIES

- 5" x 6" Walnut Hollow Farm wood tissue box
- Plasti-Kote: Classic Pearls Spray Paint - Black Basecoat, Touch of Gold Topcoat
- Delta: Black Ceramcoat acrylic paint
    Gold Gleams paint
    Decoupage medium
- 1/3 yard 1/2"-wide gold braid
- Carbon paper
- Cardboard
- Acid-free glue

See photo on page 38.

INSTRUCTIONS

1. Stuff newspaper inside tissue box, then spray three coats of black base coat over entire box.
2. Use patterns to cut eight B and four C corners out of cardboard. Fold B patterns in half. Tape one B and one C together as shown four times.
3. Place tape inside three-sided corners and place on four top corners of box. Place tape inside two-sided corners and press them on four bottom corners of box. Spray two coats of gold paint over top and sides of box. Dip end of paintbrush in gold paint and place dot on all corners as shown.
4. Crop photos. Brush one generous coat of decoupage on one side of box and center photo on surface. Press and smooth with fingers. *Note: Parts of photo may overlap corners.* Allow to dry and repeat on other three sides.
5. To finish, brush four or five coats of decoupage over all surfaces. Let dry between coats. Glue braid to inside opening at top of box.

B B

C

tape B and C together

corner C
cut 4
cardboard

corner B
cut 8
cardboard

fold line

STENCILED HEART FRAME

Design by Judy Barker for American Traditional Stencils

SUPPLIES

- American Traditional Stencil: FS-825 Cameo
- 2¾" x 8½" cream cardstock
- Art knife
- Paint: red, blue
- 3/16" stencil brush
- Embossing tool
- Light table (optional)
- Acid-free glue or Xyron Adhesive Cartridge

INSTRUCTIONS

Note: See Stenciling and Embossing General Instructions on pages 19-21.

1. Fold cardstock at 3¼" to form back and 6½" to form front, leaving 2" strip (easel). Find center of easel at 1⅜".

2. Cut two identical triangles from fold to end to form center point tab. Use art knife to make a 1/2" slit 1/4" up on back. The tab will fit into slit to create a stand.

3. Position stencil on center of front. Use low-tack tape to hold. Emboss, then stencil hearts.

4. Use art knife to cut out oval. Glue photo on back of oval.

FABRIC COVERED ALBUM

SUPPLIES

- Photo album
- 1¾ yards drapery or upholstery fabric (color of choice)
- 14½" x 25" quilt batting
- 1/2 yard rose trim
- 1/2 yard ecru double-layer gathered lace
- 2 yards ecru 1¼"-wide flat lace
- 1/2 yard ecru pearl beads
- 6¼" x 8¼" heavy cardboard
- Acid-free glue or Xyron Adhesive Cartridge

INSTRUCTIONS

1. Remove pages of album. Lay outside of book flat on batting and cut batting 1/2" larger around all edges. Glue batting on album.

2. Lay album on fabric and cut fabric 1" larger around all edges.

3. Wrap fabric to inside of album and glue down along short ends of album, keeping edges of fabric straight. Tuck batting in as you go. Glue top and bottom edges of fabric down in same way, starting in middle and working out. Cut fabric to fit around corners and glue down.

4. Cut two pieces of fabric for inside cover large enough to fit under metal center and meet but not overlap cover fabric. Spread glue under metal with knife, then use knife to push fabric under metal. Glue flat lace over raw edges, mitering or folding lace at corners.

5. Cut cardboard oval 6¼" x 8¼". Cut two layers of batting same size as oval and one layer of fabric an inch larger than oval. Place batting on cardboard, then fabric on batting. Wrap fabric around oval and glue on backside.

6. Glue double-layer gathered lace around oval on backside. Glue rose trim around oval, easing in fullness. Glue beads along edge of rose trim and glue or pin a decoration in center of oval.

7. Glue rose trim along center of spine and glue cord around edge of album.

*Design by
Marlene Maas
for Krause Publications*

CHAPTER 4

TRAVEL & VACATIONS

PARIS

SUPPLIES

- Paper Pizazz: Striped (Dots, Checks, Plaids & Stripes), Red, Blue, Yellow (Solid Jewel Tones), Letters (Pretty Alphabet Punch-Outs)
- Black paper
- Fiskars: Mini Scallop Paper Edgers
- Accu-Cut Dies: Eiffel Tower
- Acid-free glue or Xyron Adhesive Cartridge

INSTRUCTIONS

1. Trim 1/4" off each edge of striped paper and glue it on black paper.
2. Mat each photo on colored paper trimmed with Scallop edgers. Mat again on black paper.
3. Glue photos, Eiffel Tower die-cut, and punch-out letters on page.

Design by LeNae Gerig for Hot Off The Press

Design by Heidi Geffen for Sticker Planet

MAYZEE BLUFF

SUPPLIES

- Paper: black, white
- ZIG MS Markers: Black Calligraphy
- Fiskars: Deckle Paper Edgers
- The Gifted Line Stickers: Vacation
- Acid-free glue or Xyron Adhesive Cartridge

INSTRUCTIONS

1. Trim 1/4" on each edge of white paper and glue it on black paper.
2. Center sticker "Vacation" at top and apply ticket borders all around page.
3. Mat photos on black paper and trim with Deckle edgers. Arrange photos on page, and print journaling with black Calligraphy marker. Add vacation stickers.

TRAVEL CARDS

SUPPLIES

- Paper Pizazz: Cream (Plain Pastels)
- Black paper
- ZIG MS Markers: Black Calligraphy
- Fiskars: Deckle Paper Edgers
- The Gifted Line Stickers: Vacation
- Acid-free glue or Xyron Adhesive Cartridge

INSTRUCTIONS

1. Cut 6½" x 9" rectangle from black paper for each card. Fold in half.

2. Cut 4½" x 6½" rectangle from cream paper. Trim with Deckle edgers. Glue on front of black card.

3. Write message with black Calligraphy marker. Press vacation stickers on card.

Design by Heidi Geffen for Sticker Planet

TRAVEL BOX

Design by Hilary Craft for Sticker Planet

SUPPLIES

- Sandylion Sticker Designs: Sticker Paper Sheets
- Sticker Planet: full page Vacation sticker
- Wooden box
- Acid-free glue or Xyron Adhesive Cartridge

INSTRUCTIONS

1. Clean and sand box if needed. A used box will give you a nice vintage look.

2. Place stickers around box. If there are graphics or lettering on box that you don't like, just cover them with stickers.

3. Add charms or hand lettering.

JAMAICA

SUPPLIES

- Paper Pizazz: Blues, Turquoise, Purple, Greens (Plain Brights)
- White paper
- Fiskars: Paper Edgers - Wave, Clouds
- Acid-free glue or Xyron Adhesive Cartridge

INSTRUCTIONS

1. Cut papers in wide strips with Cloud and Wave edgers. Arrange strips horizontally on pages, overlapping each other. Mat photos on white paper.
2. Type journaling and cut out white paper in wavy

Design by Terina Darcey for Creating Keepsakes Magazine

design. Arrange photos, a postcard, and journaling on page. Glue in place.

Design by Heidi Geffen for Sticker Planet

INSTRUCTIONS

1. Mix and match sticker borders across top and bottom of white paper.
2. Use circle cutter to crop photos and mats. Cut sun freehand to add bright mat behind photo.
3. Mat square photo with colored paper trimmed with Deckle edgers for postcard effect. Add postage stamp for fun.

LONGBOAT KEY

SUPPLIES

- Paper Pizazz: Yellow, Orange, Purple, Blue (Plain Brights)
- White paper
- Fiskars: Circle Cutter, Deckle Paper Edgers
- ZIG MS Markers: Clean Color - Cobalt Blue, Yellow, Purple
  Calligraphy - Baby Blue
  Opaque Extra-Fine - White
  Millennium .05mm Black
- Sandylion Stickers: Summer Fun Border, Winter Activities Border, Pooh Border, Fish
- Sticker Planet Pop-Dots
- Acid-free glue or Xyron Adhesive Cartridge

4. Add stickers along side to create colorful border. Apply Pop-Dots under some bubbles to add dimension to page.
5. Journal using brightly colored markers. Add accents on bubbles with white opaque marker.

HAWAIIAN VACATION

Design by LeNae Gerig for Hot Off The Press

SUPPLIES

- Paper Pizazz: Ferns (Great Outdoors), Red, Orange, Blue (Plain Brights)
- Vacation punch-outs
- Fiskars: Colonial Paper Edgers
- ZIG MS Markers: Writers - Black, Red, Green
- Templates: oval, circle
- Acid-free glue or Xyron Adhesive Cartridge

INSTRUCTIONS

1. Triple mat largest photo on red, orange, and blue paper, trimming red with Colonial edgers. Make orange mat wider and blue mat very thin.

2. Use templates to trim one photo in oval shape and other in circle. Mat both photos. Trim with Colonial edgers. Silhouette vehicle and mat it.

3. Create journaling triangle with orange and red paper trimmed with edgers. Journal with different colored markers.

4. Arrange photos, triangle, and vacation punch-outs on fern background. Glue in place. Cut four red triangle photo corners and glue on corners of largest photo.

TRAVEL TIPS

- Number the photo canisters before you leave on your trip. Transfer the numbers to the photo processing envelopes when you take the photos to be developed.
- Replace batteries with fresh ones right before you begin your trip.
- Carry a small notebook for journaling. Take brief notes on where you go and what you see. Add more thorough diary entries each night before you go to sleep.
- Pick up postcards to add to your own photos. They are usually great pictures that you couldn't possibly take yourself.
- Put your album together as soon as you retun from your trip while the details are still fresh in your mind.

TRIP UP NORTH

Design by Kate Stephani for Krause Publications

SUPPLIES

- Paper Pizazz: Wood Scene (Great Outdoors), Brown, Blue, Mauve, Green (Solid Jewel Tones), Cream (Plain Pastels)
- Fiskars: Paper Edgers - Ripple, Clouds, Notch
- ZIG MS Markers: Writers - Black, Green
- Accu-Cut Dies: Evergreen
- Oval template
- Acid-free glue or Xyron Adhesive Cartridge

INSTRUCTIONS

1. Crop photos in variety of shapes, having one larger than others for center of interest. Double and triple mat photos.

2. Cut rectangles from cream paper for journaling. Mat on darker paper. Make one rectangle look like sign by cutting a post from brown paper.

3. Arrange photos, journaling and die-cut on page. Glue in place. Make four large triangle corners and glue on one photo. Add dot and stitch-line accents.

OUR CAMPING TRIP

SUPPLIES

- ❧ Paper Pizazz: Wooded Scene (Great Outdoors), 2 Greens (Plain Brights), Great Outdoors Cutouts
- ❧ Fiskars: Aztec Paper Edgers, Tree Punch
- ❧ ZIG MS Markers: Black Calligraphy
- ❧ Acid-free glue or Xyron Adhesive Cartridge

INSTRUCTIONS

1. Use Aztec edgers to trim wooded scene paper 1/2" from each edge. Glue paper at an angle on bright green paper. Trim edges even.

2. Trim two rectangular photos with same edgers and mat on plain paper trimmed with edgers. Mat again on dark green paper and trim.

3. Use circle template to crop smaller photo, then mat in same way.

4. Glue matted photos on page. Glue on moose cutout. Punch small trees from dark green paper. Glue on page. Journal with black Calligraphy pen.

Design by LeNae Gerig for Hot Off The Press

FOUR CORNERS

SUPPLIES

- Paper Pizazz: Blue, Gray (Solid Jewel Tones), Orange (Plain Brights)
- White paper
- ZIG MS Markers: Black Fine & Chisel Writer
- Fiskars: Alligator Paper Edgers, Circle Cutter
- Accu-Cut Dies: Traveler
- Map
- Acid-free glue or Xyron Adhesive Cartridge

INSTRUCTIONS

1. Cut four photos in circles with circle cutter. Double mat them on gray, then on orange paper. Trim with Alligator edgers. Crop rectangular photo and double mat on gray, then on white paper.

2. Cut headline from map (or color photocopy) using Traveler die-cuts.

3. Position photos and headlines on page, placing cropped photos over some letters to add dimension. Add tiny orange corner on page trimmed with edgers.

4. Add details and journaling with black markers. Outline headline letters with black marker.

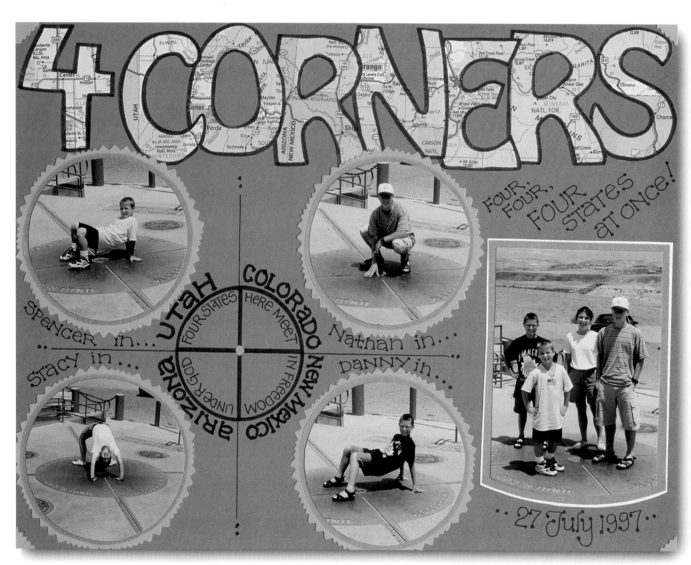

Design by Carol Snyder for EK Success

DISNEYLAND

SUPPLIES

- Paper Pizazz: Pink (Plain Pastels), Pink, Blue (Plain Brights)
- Fiskars: Disney's Playtime with Mickey and Friends
- ZIG MS Markers: Pink Calligraphy
  Writers - Black, Red, Yellow
- Acid-free glue or Xyron Adhesive Cartridge

INSTRUCTIONS

1. Cut frame 1/4"- wide from bright pink paper. Glue on blue paper.

2. Cut one light and one bright pink rectangle same size as each cropped photo. Draw stitch marks around edges of rectangles with small end of Calligraphy pen. Draw black line down one side of each stitch mark.

3. Place rectangles behind photos so they are offset. Glue in place on page. Cut out Minnie and glue on page.

4. Use black Writer to draw squiggly lines and dots around outside edge of each photo. Add stitch lines to corner of photos. Write words using pink Calligraphy marker. Accent letters with black Writer. Draw hearts around Minnie with black marker and color in with pink and yellow markers.

5. Draw hearts in corners and middle of sides on frame. Color

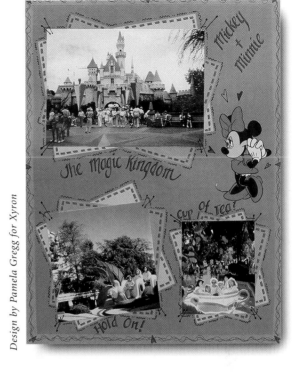

Design by Pamela Gregg for Xyron

with pink Calligraphy marker. Connect hearts with one squiggly pink line and two squiggly black lines.

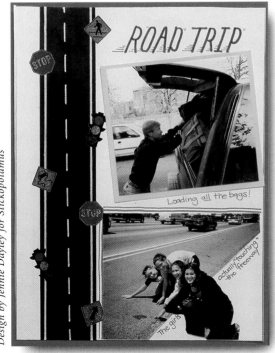

Design by Jennie Dayley for Stickopotamus

ROAD TRIP

SUPPLIES

- Paper Pizazz: Red, Yellow (Plain Brights)
- Cardstock: black, white
- ZIG MS Markers: Writers - Red, Green
  Red Scroll & Brush
  White Fine Writer
- Stickopotamus Stickers: Traffic Signs
- Acid-free glue or Xyron Adhesive Cartridge

INSTRUCTIONS

1. Cut 1¾" strip of black paper. Draw road lines with white opaque marker.

2. Trim edges of white paper 1/8" on each side. Mat on red paper. Glue black road vertically on one side of white paper. Arrange stickers along roadsides.

3. Mat one photo on yellow paper.

4. Use scroll end of red marker to create double-line border around other photo. Print journaling with red and green markers. Use fine-tip of Writer to make action marks that make title look as if it's racing off page.

CHAPTER 5

BABIES

Design by Judy Barker for American Traditional Stencils

BABY GIFT CARD

SUPPLIES

- American Traditional Stencils: FS-825 Cameo, FS-946 Bouncing Baby
- Paints of choice: red, yellow, blue, green
- 3½" x 5" cream cardstock
- Fiskars: Rounder Corner Edgers
- Light table or alternative light source
- Embossing tool
- 1/4" stencil brush
- Art knife
- Masking tape
- Acid-free glue or Xyron Adhesive Cartridge

INSTRUCTIONS

Note: See Stenciling and Embossing General Instructions on pages 19-21.

1. Fold card in half to 2½" x 3½". Place cameo stencil on front of card. Secure with two small pieces of masking tape.

2. Place stencil down on light source and emboss oval. Cut out oval with art knife.

3. Stencil parts of baby stencil on corners of card. Use masking tape to block out any design you don't want to stencil. Mix colors by blending on palette.

IT'S A GIRL

Design by Toni Nelson for
EK Success

SUPPLIES

- Paper Pizazz: Pastel Stripes (Baby), Pink (Plain Brights)
- White paper
- Fiskars: Swivel Knife, Scallop Paper Edgers
- Border Buddy: #4 Holiday
- ZIG MS Markers:
    Extra-Fine White Opaque Writer
    Fine Pink Opaque Writer
- Stickopotamus Stickers: It's a Girl!
- Circle paper punch
- 6" white 1/8"-wide ribbon
- Acid-free glue or Xyron Adhesive Cartridge

INSTRUCTIONS

1. Trace bubble template on back of striped paper and cut out with swivel knife, creating 2¼"-wide space. Glue strip of pink paper behind space. Draw stitch lines and dots along pink edges with white Opaque Writer.
2. Mat photos on pink paper. Cut pink rectangle for journaling. Glue photos and rectangle on page.
3. Print journaling. Add stickers and doodles.
4. For candy bar, remove wrapper and use it as pattern to trace on striped paper. Trace bubble template on side edges of paper and cut out. Wrap candy with striped wrapper. Cut white rectangle for journaling and trim with Scallop edgers. Mat on pink paper. Print message with pink Opaque Writer. Glue rectangle on front of wrapper.
5. For gift tag, cut 2" x 3" rectangle. Cut strip of striped paper using bubble template and cut out. Glue strip on rectangle. Glue 1/2"-wide pink strip of paper down center of striped strip. Print message with white Opaque Writer. Punch hole in one corner. Insert 6" length of ribbon through hole and attach to gift.

ROSES BABY CARD

Design by Julie McGuffee for Accu-Cut

SUPPLIES

- Paper Pizazz: Yellow (Plain Pastels), Yellow Plaid (Light Great Backgrounds)
- Cards with Pizazz: Yellow Roses
- Fiskars: Paper Crimper
- ZIG MS Markers: White Fine Opaque Writer
- Accu-Cut Dies: Card Template, Oval, Oval Picture Frame
- 8" white 1/4"-wide satin ribbon
- Circle paper punch
- Vellum
- Acid-free glue or Xyron Adhesive Cartridge

INSTRUCTIONS

1. Cut piece of vellum and piece of plaid paper same size as front of card.
2. Trim sides of vellum with scalloped border die, then cut oval from center. Crimp vellum with paper crimper.
3. Cut oval in front of card and glue vellum on front.
4. Punch two holes in top of oval. Thread ribbon through holes and tie in bow.

5. Glue plaid paper on inside of card facing front opening.
6. Mat photo with oval picture-frame die-cut. Glue on plaid paper, centering it in opening on front of card.
7. Make small dot accents around edge of mat with white Opaque Writer.

TUBBY TIME
& SPLISH SPLASH

SUPPLIES

- ❧ Paper Pizazz: Big Bubbles, (Childhood), Tiny Bubbles (Baby), Yellow, Blue (Plain Brights)
- ❧ White paper
- ❧ Border Buddy: #4 Holiday
- ❧ Fiskars: Swivel Knife, Clouds Paper Edgers
- ❧ ZIG MS Markers: Writers - Baby Blue, Yellow
- ❧ Stickopotamus Stickers: Bath Time
- ❧ Acid-free glue or Xyron Adhesive Cartridge

Designs by Toni Nelson for EK Success

INSTRUCTIONS

1. Trace bubble border on back of large bubble paper, 1" in on all four sides. Carefully cut out along line with swivel knife.

2. Glue bubble frame on one white paper and inside bubble cutout on another white paper.

3. Use bubble edge of Border Buddy to draw border inside or outside paper border with blue and yellow Writers.

4. Mount photos on tiny bubble paper and trim with Clouds edgers. Mat again on yellow paper. Cut white rectangle for journaling. Mat on yellow, then tiny bubble paper. Trim with same edgers. Mat again on yellow paper.

5. Glue photos and rectangle on pages. Print journaling. Press stickers in place and add pen accents.

Seven Months

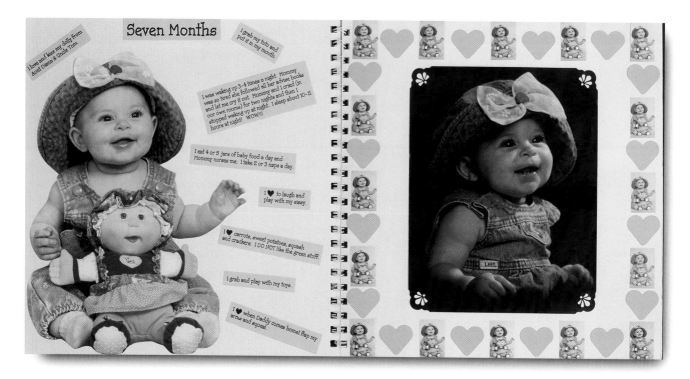

Design by Stephanie Barnard for Memory Makers Magazine

Supplies

- Paper Pizazz: Blue (Plain Pastels)
- Accu-Cut Dies: Small Heart
- Decorative corner punch
- Ruler
- Acid-free glue or Xyron Adhesive Cartridge

Instructions

1. Crop large photo in silhouette and glue on page.
2. Type title and other bits of information and print on colored paper. Cut text into rectangular shapes and arrange around photo. Glue in place.
3. For second page, arrange wallet-size photos and pink heart die-cuts around edges of page, using ruler to space them evenly. Glue in place.
4. Trim corners of large photo with decorative corner punch. Glue photo on page.

MADISON

SUPPLIES

- Paper Pizazz: Purple Plaid & Stripes (Dots, Checks, Plaids & Stripes), Pink, Lavender (Plain Pastels), Purple (Solid Muted Colors)
- Fiskars: Paper Edgers - Deckle, Cloud
- ZIG MS Markers: Purple Writer
- Templates: circle, oval, heart
- Acid-free glue or Xyron Adhesive Cartridge

INSTRUCTIONS

1. Trim plaid paper 1/2" along each edge and mat on purple paper. Trim with Cloud edgers. Glue at an angle on striped paper and trim edges even.
2. Crop one photo with circle template and one with oval. Double mat photos on lavender, then pink paper. Trim with Deckle edgers or straight scissors.
3. Glue photos on page, overlapping some to create pattern for eye to follow.
4. Cut out hearts for journaling and for decoration. Glue on page.

Design by Becky Goughnour for Hot Off The Press

Design by Jenny Curtis for Creating Keepsakes Magazine

GOING IN CIRCLES

SUPPLIES

- Paper Pizazz: Pink, Turquoise (Plain Brights), Purple (Solid Jewel Tones)
- White paper
- Fiskars: Circle Cutter
- Inspire Graphics: Lettering Delights
- Acid-free glue or Xyron Adhesive Cartridge

INSTRUCTIONS

Overlapping circles matted with different colors are a great space-saver and a perfect tie-in for the "going in circles" phrase. Cut a white rectangle for journaling and mat on purple paper.

WATCH ME GROW

Design by Joyce Schweizer for Memory Makers Magazine

SUPPLIES

- Paper Pizazz: Pink, Blue, Yellow (Plain Pastels)
- Pink parchment paper
- Fiskars: Scallop Paper Edgers
- ZIG MS Markers: Writers - Black, Pink
- Circle template
- Giraffe pattern
- Stickers
- Acid-free glue or Xyron Adhesive Cartridge

INSTRUCTIONS

1. Trace giraffe on page using pattern and light table.

2. Crop photos using circle template. Mat each photo on colored paper. Trim with Scallop paper edgers.

3. Write title with pink Writer. Add height and weight information with black Writer.

4. Add stickers as accents around title and photos.

MISS TABITHA

SUPPLIES

- Paper Pizazz: Cream, Pink (Plain Pastels), Burgundy (Solid Jewel Tones)
- Fiskars: Circle Cutter with Mat
  Victorian Paper Edgers
  5" Micro-Tip Scissors
  McCall's Remember the Years™ 1940-1949 Papers
- ZIG MS Markers: Burgundy Writer
- Necklace clip art
- Pencil
- Acid-free glue or Xyron Adhesive Cartridge

INSTRUCTIONS

1. Cut out circle of flowered certificate, cutting around or "bumping out" four roses.

2. Position photo under certificate page and lightly mark where subject in photo overlaps circle (or part of subject you want to extend beyond cutout circle).

3. Cut out marked area, making sure not to cut beyond marked area of photo. Gently pull cutout of subject out of circle. Glue photo in place.

4. Crop three head photos with circle cutter. Cut mats from contrasting colored circles in sizes that increase in increments of 1/4". Two photos have double mats and third has four mats. Trim some edges of circles with Victorian edgers. Glue circle photos on page.

5. Necklace is color photocopy. Mat necklace and glue in place. Write journaling with burgundy Writer.

MOLLY

SUPPLIES

- Paper Pizazz: Green Checks, Dots (Dots, Checks, Plaids & Stripes), Peach (Plain Pastels)
- White paper
- ZIG MS Markers: Black Writer
- Accu-Cut Dies: Rattle
- Acid-free glue or Xyron Adhesive Cartridge

INSTRUCTIONS

1. Mat photos on peach paper. For each photo, cut slightly larger shape from plaid paper and mat on white. Turn mats and glue photos on them. Glue matted photos on page.

2. For corners, cut four triangles from plaid paper. Glue thin strip of plaid paper along bottom edge. Glue corners on page.

3. For rattle, cut rattle from peach and white paper. Cut rattle apart and glue back together with white handle. Cut strip of plaid paper and glue across middle of rattle. Print journaling with black Writer. Glue rattle on page.

Design by LeNae Gerig for Hot Off The Press

Design by Fiskars, Inc.

CHAPTER 6

HOLIDAYS

EASTER EGG HUNT

INSTRUCTIONS

1. Use Border Buddy to trace scallop edge around white paper. Cut along outside of border and glue on floral paper. Use bullet tip of hyacinth Writer to make dots around scallop edge.

2. Mat large photo on white, then purple paper. Crop other photo in oval and mat on purple paper. Glue photos on page.

3. Nestle decorative egg stickers in slit of die-cut basket. Glue basket on page.

4. Before gluing down die-cut grass, overlap jelly bean, egg and chick stickers through strands of grass so they appear to be hiding, not just sitting on top. Glue grass on bottom of page.

5. Print title on page with blue jay marker. Journal along sides of photos with hyacinth Writer.

Design by Jennie Dayley for Stickopotamus

SUPPLIES

- Paper Pizazz: Purple (Solid Jewel Tones), Yellow (Plain Brights) Purple Flowers (Floral Papers)
- White cardstock
- ZIG MS Markers: Hyacinth Writer, Blue Jay Fine & Chisel
- Accu-Cut Dies: Basket, Grass
- Border Buddy Jr: Party
- Stickopotamus Stickers: Easter Eggs, Jelly Beans
- Acid-free glue or Xyron Adhesive Cartridge

FOURTH OF JULY

INSTRUCTIONS

1. Crop two photos using oval and circle templates. Mat on white paper and trim with Scallop edgers. Mat again on patterned paper and use straight edge scissors to cut rectangle or square. Mat on white and trim with edgers.

2. Double mat one photo on patterned paper, then on white. Trim with edgers. Cut white square for journaling and mat on patterned paper, then white. Trim with edgers.

3. Glue photos and journal square on page. Glue on stars and firecracker die-cuts.

4. Journal and add squiggle lines and dots for accents with black Writer.

SUPPLIES

- Paper Pizazz: Dots, Stripes, Stars (Dots, Checks, Plaids & Stripes), Gold (Plain Brights)
- White paper
- ZIG MS Markers: Black Writer
- Fiskars: Mini Scallop Paper Edgers
- Accu-Cut Dies: Star, Firecracker
- Circle and oval template
- Acid-free glue or Xyron Adhesive Cartridge

Design by LeNae Gerig for Hot Off The Press

Halloween

Design by Jean Kievlan for Accu-Cut

Supplies

- Paper Pizazz: Gray, Green (Soft Muted Colors), Orange (Plain Brights) Tan (Plain Pastels), Spider (Holiday Punch-Outs)
- White paper
- ZIG MS Markers: Writers - Black, Green
- Accu-Cut Dies: Small Pumpkin #3, Small Cat, Small Ghost, Grass Border, Small Sign
- Stickopotamus Stickers: Star
- Acid-free glue or Xyron Adhesive Cartridge

Instructions

1. Cut cat from black and gray paper and ghost from white paper using dies.
2. For hinge at top of pumpkin, fold orange paper in half. Position fold just below stem on pumpkin die and cut pumpkin.
3. Fold 8½" x 11" piece of green paper in half and in half again. Cut all four sides with grass border die. Mat three photos on grass borders.
4. Silhouette photo to place in grass and photo in pumpkin pop-up.
5. Cut white rectangle for journaling. Write title with black and green Writers. Arrange on page with die-cuts, photos and spider punch-out. Glue in place. Write captions. Apply star stickers randomly on page.

THANKSGIVING

SUPPLIES

- ❧ Paper Pizazz: Torn Paper (Inspirations & Celebrations), Brown, Green (Solid Muted Colors)
- ❧ Fiskars: Ripple Paper Edgers
- ❧ ZIG MS Markers: Black Writer
- ❧ Acid-free glue or Xyron Adhesive Cartridge

INSTRUCTIONS

1. Mat photos on brown paper and trim with Ripple edgers. Mat again on green paper. Cut brown rectangle for journaling and mat in same way.

2. Arrange photos and rectangle on page and glue in place.

3. Print title and date to finish this heartwarming page.

Design by Becky Goughnour for Hot Off The Press

Design by LeNae Gerig for Hot Off The Press

CHRISTMAS PORTRAIT

SUPPLIES

- ❧ Paper Pizazz: Music Sheets (Romantic Papers), Rust, Green, (Solid Jewel Tones), Tan (Plain Pastels)
- ❧ Fiskars: Seagull Paper Edgers
- ❧ Large oval template
- ❧ Circle paper punch

INSTRUCTIONS

1. Crop large photo using oval template. Glue on rust paper and trim with Seagull edgers. Punch holes around mat, spacing them evenly. Glue on tan paper and cut in same way. Glue on green paper and trim with edgers. Mat smaller photo on rust and trim with edgers. Mat on tan, then green paper.

2. Trim 1/2" off patterned paper on all edges with edgers. Mat on rust and trim in same way. Glue on green paper. Arrange and glue photos on patterned paper.

TROPICAL CHRISTMAS

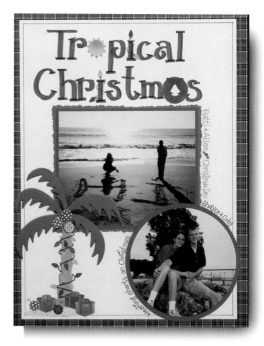

SUPPLIES

- Paper Pizazz: Red, Green (Plain Brights), Christmas Plaid (Christmas)
- White paper
- ZIG MS Markers: Fine & Chisel - Red, Green
  Pine Green Fine Opaque Writer
- Fiskars: Circle Cutter, Deckle Edge Scissors
- Accu-Cut Dies: Palm Tree
- Stickopotamus Stickers: Christmas Accessories, Shore
- Acid-free glue or Xyron Adhesive Cartridge

INSTRUCTIONS

1. Trim 1/4" off all sides of white paper and glue on plaid paper. Draw straight line border 1/8" in from edge of white paper.

2. Crop one photo in a circle. Mat both photos on red paper. Mat larger photo on green and trim with Deckle edgers. Glue photos on page.

3. Print title on page with green Fine & Chisel marker and highlight letters with red. For added touch, use

Design by Jennie Dayley for Stickopotamus

stickers to replace some letters.

4. Cut palm tree from tan and green paper. Cut and glue green palm branches on tan tree trunk. Use pine green Opaque Writer to draw cord around trunk of palm tree. Add Christmas light stickers on cord and sticker presents under tree. Hang sticker ornaments on palm tree.

5. Journal along photos with red and green Fine & Chisel markers.

GREEN ORNAMENT GREETING CARD

SUPPLIES

- Cards with Pizazz: Red and Green Stripes
- ZIG MS Markers: Copper Penny Extra-Fine Opaque Writer
- Accu-Cut Dies: Christmas Ornament #3, Mini Bow
- Green and red shiny (mirro) paper
- Magnetic sheet
- Acid-free glue or Xyron Adhesive Cartridge

INSTRUCTIONS

1. Glue the shiny green paper to magnet sheet and cut out ornament shape.

2. Cut mini bow from red shiny paper and glue on top of ornament. Glue photo in opening.

3. Write message on front of ornament with gold Opaque Writer.

Design by Julie McGuffee for Accu-Cut

4. Fold card with pattern to inside. Fold front of card in half back towards center fold. Glue ornament on front of card so it overlaps fold as shown. The ornament can be removed and used as refrigerator magnet.

BETHLEHEM

Design by Kim McCrary for Creating Keepsakes Magazine

SUPPLIES

- Paper Pizazz: Blue (Solid Jewel Tones), Tan (Plain Pastels), Gold Metallic (Pearlescent)
- White paper
- ZIG MS Markers: Opaque Gold Metallic Writer
- Fiskars: Paper Trimmer
- Mrs. Grossman's Stickers: Lamb
- Paper punches: holly, star, circle
- Acid-free glue or Xyron Adhesive Cartridge

INSTRUCTIONS

1. Cut two white rectangles for journaling. Mat rectangles and photo on gold metallic paper. Cut out large star and rays from gold paper.

2. For manger, cut eight 1/2" x 4½" tan strips with paper trimmer.

3. Arrange items on blue paper and glue in place. Journal with gold Opaque Writer. Make small dots on manger for nails.

4. Punch out stars, holly and berries and glue on page. Add lamb stickers.

CHAPTER 5

SPORTS

GOLFING

SUPPLIES

- Paper Pizazz: Golf Balls (Sports)
- Paper: white, black
- Fiskars: Paper Edgers - Stamp, Scallop Nostalgia Corner Edgers
- Templates: circle, oval
- Acid-free glue or Xyron Adhesive Cartridge

INSTRUCTIONS

1. Cut 1/2" from each side of golf ball paper. Mat on black paper. Crop one photo in circle and another in oval. Cut one rectangular picture with Nostalgia corner edgers. Mat three photos on white, then black.

2. Trim one photo mat with Scallop edgers. Cut corners on other photo mats to match photo. Save black corners. Mat oval photo on black and trim with Scallop edgers.

3. Type journaling and cut white paper in rectangle. Mat on black paper and trim with Stamp edgers. Mat again on white, then black paper.

4. Arrange photos and rectangle on page. Glue in place. Glue black corners close to photo with decorative corners, leaving a small space.

Dave Larson
Iola Country Club
Iola, WI
August 21, 1998

Design by Julie Stephani for Krause Publications

POP-UP SOCCER

Design by Julie McGuffee for Accu-Cut

SUPPLIES

- Paper Pizazz: Green (Solid Muted Tones), Soccer Ball (Sports), Green (Plain Brights), Border Punch-Outs - Sports Balls
- Green cardstock
- ZIG MS Markers: Writers - Black, Green
- Accu-Cut Dies: Megaphone, Grass Border, Card Template, Oval, Deckle Border, Small Pop Up
- Acid-free glue or Xyron Adhesive Cartridge

INSTRUCTIONS

Note: See Pop-Up General Instructions on page 22.
1. Cut one grass border on folded paper. Use to hinge two pieces of green background paper together. Cut additional grass borders for sides of pages and to mat one photo.
2. Glue photos, die-cuts, punch-out borders and shapes on page.

3. Cut card from card template. Cut oval in front of card for photo. Trim front edge of card with Deckle edgers. Glue photo in opening. Journal on front and inside of card with black and green Writers. Glue card on page.
4. Glue punch-outs on megaphone. Glue megaphone along top of hinged green pop-up. Glue pop-up on page.

TRACK MEET

Design by Carol Snyder for EK Success

SUPPLIES

- Paper Pizazz: Brown, Blue, Tan (Solid Muted Colors), Green (Plain Brights), Cream paper (Plain Pastels)
- ZIG MS Markers: Writers - Black, Blue, Green, Yellow White Chisel Opaque Writer
- Fiskars: Jigsaw Paper Edgers
- Acid-free glue or Xyron Adhesive Cartridge

INSTRUCTIONS

1. Fold page-size piece of scrap paper in quarters and cut out template of track ring to fit scrapbook page. Use folded method to insure that you create a symmetrical track ring. Trace and cut from brown paper. Draw lane lines using narrow end of white Opaque Writer. Mat track ring on tan paper.

2. Using track pattern, trace and cut out inner field from green paper. Glue in center of track ring. For corners, cut four triangles from green paper and four from blue paper. Use Jigsaw edgers to trim long edges to

resemble track shoes. Glue green over blue and glue in corners.

3. Print words "Track Meet" on beige paper, tracing "T" from Sports Alphabet. Color in sneaker and add green lines for grass. Cut out words in silhouette and glue on page.

4. Cut photos in ovals and mat on blue paper trimmed with Jigsaw edgers. Glue on page.

5. Add journaling and stitch lines around track with black Writer.

SPORTS ALPHABET

Designs by Carol Snyder for EK Success

SPORTS WORDS

SUPPLIES

- Paper: white, colored or patterned paper for matting
- ZIG MS Markers:
  Black Writer
  Writers - colors of choice
  Earth Color Memory Pencils
- Acid-free glue or Xyron Adhesive Cartridge

INSTRUCTIONS

1. Select letters from Sports Alphabet. Trace letters using light table.

2. Ink thin lines with fine point and dark lines with larger point of Writer.

3. Color in letters with color pencils or color Writers.

"Y" NOT GO BOWLING

SUPPLIES

- ❧ Paper Pizazz: Red, Blue, Orange (Plain Brights)
- ❧ Paper: black, white
- ❧ ZIG MS Markers: Writers - Black, Red
  Earth Color Memory Pencils
- ❧ Fiskars: Regal Corner Edgers, Pinking Paper Edgers
- ❧ Stickopotamus Stickers: Bowling
- ❧ Acid-free glue or Xyron Adhesive Cartridge

Design by Carol Snyder for EK Success

INSTRUCTIONS

1. Cut white rectangle for journaling. Cut out the letter "Y" from blue paper and glue on rectangle. Print title, tracing a "B" from the Sports Alphabet on page 69. If desired, add dimension to each bowling ball by coloring it in with gray Memory Pencil. Mat rectangle on black paper. Trim with Pinking edgers.
2. Trim corners of each picture with Regal corner edgers. Mat two photos with blue or orange paper and trim corners.
3. Glue photos and rectangle on page.
4. Add journaling, using stickers to take place of letters. Add stickers on corners. Draw straight line around page. Make dots at ends of lines.

ALL STAR BASEBALL

SUPPLIES

- ❧ Paper Pizazz: Balls (Sports), Red, Green, (Plain Brights), Green (Solid Muted Colors), Border Punch Outs - Balls
- ❧ White paper
- ❧ Fiskars: Circle Cutter, Circle Punch
- ❧ ZIG MS Markers: Writers - Black, Red
- ❧ Accu-Cut Dies: Ball, Bat and Glove, Grass Border, Circle, Small Star #3, Marshmallow Alphabet
- ❧ Stickopotamus Stickers: Sports
- ❧ Acid-free glue or Xyron Adhesive Cartridge

INSTRUCTIONS

1. Cut letters from ball paper and red paper. Glue them together having red offset. Cut die-cuts from appropriate paper.
2. Crop two photos with circle cutter. Mat on ball paper. Silhouette two other photos. Arrange photos, punch-outs and die-cuts on green paper. Glue in place.

Design by Julie McGuffee for Accu-Cut

3. For small balls, punch circles from white paper. Make stitch lines with red Writer. Journal on large baseball with black and red Writers.

NASCAR

Design by Becky Goughnour for Hot Off The Press

SUPPLIES

- Paper Pizazz: Racing Flags (Masculine Papers), Orange (Plain Brights), Solid Jewel Tones, Masculine Papers Cutouts
- Paper: white, black
- Fiskars: Zipper Paper Edgers
- ZIG MS Markers: Black Writer
- Circle template
- Acid-free glue or Xyron Adhesive Cartridge

INSTRUCTIONS

1. Trim 1/4" off each side of flag paper and glue on orange paper.

2. Mat rectangular photo on white, then black paper. Trim with Zipper edgers.

3. Use template to cut another photo in circle. Mat on white, then black paper.

4. Trim around photo of car and mat on white paper, creating sunburst effect around car. Mat again on black paper.

5. Glue photos on page, overlapping them to create a flow. Glue on car cutout.

6. Type or print journaling on white paper. Cut paper in shape of two flags. Mat on black paper, adding pole on each flag.

HIKING IN NEW MEXICO

Design by Carol Snyder for EK Success

SUPPLIES

- Paper Pizazz: Tan (Plain Pastels), Brown, Green, Moss (Solid Muted Colors)
- ZIG MS Markers: Writers - Black, Brown
- Fiskars: Art Deco Corner Edgers
- Accu-Cut Dies: Traveler
- Inkworx Air Art Gun
- Acid-free glue or Xyron Adhesive Cartridge

INSTRUCTIONS

1. Trim corners of photos with Art Deco corner edgers, saving trimmed off pieces. Position photos on tan paper and mark placement with light pencil marks.

2. Use extra scenery photos to cut die-cut letters "N" and "M". Print headline on tan paper with black Writer and glue die-cut letters in place. Accent letters with fine tip of black Writer.

3. Cut and rip paper of rocks and fallen log. Add dimension to rocks by spraying with Inkworx gun. Draw bark details with brown Writer.

4. Glue rocks and log in place. For fallen bits of bark on bottom of log, cut thin pieces from brown paper and glue in place.

5. Cut thin blades of grass from green paper and glue on page. Tear clumps of moss from green paper and glue on log and rock. Draw detail grass lines and dots for dirt with black Writer.

6. Glue photos in positions marked on page. Glue corner pieces close to photos. Print journaling and draw two straight lines around border of page with brown

MOLIKINI, HAWAII

Design by Julie McGuffee for Accu-Cut

SUPPLIES

- Paper Pizazz: Blue, Peach, Green , Turquoise, Gold (Plain Pastels), Little Mermaid Paper and Cutouts
- White paper
- Fiskars: Dragonback Paper Edgers
- ZIG MS Markers: Black Calligraphy, Black Writer
- Accu-Cut Dies: Border #170, Frame, Small Seahorse, Mini Fish, Small Shell #1
- Stickopotamus Stickers: The Shore
- Acid-free glue or Xyron Adhesive Cartridge

INSTRUCTIONS

1. Stack three shades of blue paper together for ocean. Cut border toward top of sheets. Glue first sheet to background paper and turn second sheet in opposite direction and place on background paper about 2" further down from first. Place third sheet on top of second (don't turn this sheet) about 2" further down. Don't glue second or third sheets. Trim bottom edges of paper even with background sheet.

2. Fold top sheet to right of background sheet and next sheet to left. Align bottom edges even with background sheet and sides so they join background sheet. Cut shell die-cuts for hinges. Glue on background and adjoining sheets of paper

3. Bump, crop and mat photos. Glue photos on both sides of hinged paper and background. Decorate with additional die-cut shapes, cutouts and stickers.

4. Journal and add decorative edges around photos with black markers.

CHAPTER 8

KIDS

T IS FOR TAYLOR

SUPPLIES

- Paper Pizazz: Blue Plaid (Dots, Checks, Plaids & Stripes), Green (Plain Brights)
- White paper
- Border Buddy: #3 Geo, Border Buddy Jr. - Geometric
- Fiskars: Swivel Knife, Circle Cutter
- ZIG MS Markers:
    Writers - Green, Blue
    Fine & Chisel - Green, Blue
- Stickopotamus Stickers: any "T" stickers
- Acid-free glue or Xyron Adhesive Cartridge

Design by Toni Nelson for EK Success

INSTRUCTIONS

1. Make window border with mini zigzag edge of Border Buddy 3. Trace on backside of green paper and cut out with scissors or swivel knife. Glue border on white paper. Use same edge to trace border on back of plaid paper to make 2½" x 10½" rectangle for journaling. Cut and glue rectangle just above bottom border.
2. Use bullet tip of Border Buddy Jr. to create mini zigzag border on white paper above plaid rectangle with green Fine marker. Draw letters in corners with blue Chisel marker. Connect corner letters with green straight lines and write "T" words on lines with blue Writer.
3. Write title (T is for Taylor) on 1¾" x 9½" white rectangle with green Chisel marker. Add blue accent lines. Glue on plaid paper.
4. Crop photos (one with circle cutter) and glue on page. Add stickers that begin with "T' and print labels with blue Writer.

H IS FOR HANNAH

Design by Toni Nelson for EK Success

SUPPLIES

- White paper
- Border Buddy Jr.: Geometric
- Fiskars: Circle Cutter
- ZIG MS Markers:
    Writers - Pink, Orange
    Calligraphy - Orange
- Stickopotamus Stickers: any "H" stickers
- Acid-free glue or Xyron Adhesive Cartridge

INSTRUCTIONS

1. Use bullet tip of Border Buddy Jr. to create mini scallop border on page with pink Writer. Draw letters in two corners with broad tip of orange Calligraphy pen. Connect corner letters with straight pink lines and write "H" words with orange on lines.

2. Crop photos (two with circle cutter) and glue on page. Add stickers that begin with "H" and print labels with pink Writer. Add dots and doodles.

WENDY

Design by Becky Goughnour for Hot Off The Press

SUPPLIES

- Paper Pizazz: Baby's Things, Polka-Dot (Baby), Pink, Blue, Yellow (Plain Pastels), Baby Punch-Outs
- Fiskars: Jigsaw Paper Edgers, Rounder Corner Edgers
- Letter stickers
- Templates: oval, round
- Acid-free glue or Xyron Adhesive Cartridge

INSTRUCTIONS

1. Cut 3"-wide strip of pink paper and trim with Jigsaw edgers. Mat on blue then yellow. Glue on right side of page.

2. Round corners of three photos with Rounder corner edgers. Mat on polka-dot paper. Round corners and glue on strip.

3. Crop other photos using oval and round templates.

Mat on yellow then polka-dot paper and trim with Jigsaw edgers. Mat one photo on blue and one photo on pink. Glue on page. Add punch-outs.

4. Place sticker letters on colored paper and cut into squares. Arrange letters and punch-outs on page. Glue in place.

FOUR-PHOTO FRAME

Design by Posh Impressions for Xyron

- Paper Pizazz: tapestry (Pretty Papers)
- Mat board
- Fiskars: Swivel Knife
- Templates: circle, oval, square, rectangle
- Acid-free glue or Xyron Adhesive Cartridge

INSTRUCTIONS

1. From mat board cut one 8" x 8½" (backing), two 3½" x 8" (frames). Score larger piece and fold in half. Trace templates an equal distance from sides of frames. Cut out openings.

2. Cut piece of paper 1/2" larger all around than each mat board piece, including frame openings.

3. For backing lining, cut piece of paper same size as backing. Glue on inside of backing. Glue larger paper on outside of backing. Fold paper over edges and glue on inside of backing, mitering corners to fit.

4. For each frame, fold paper over outside edges and glue to inside same as for backing. For openings, make slits 1/4" apart on oval and circle or in corners of square and rectangle. Fold paper over edges and glue to inside of frame. See illustration.

5. *Option: cut scrap of clear laminate or acetate for each frame opening. Cut to fit 1/4" past openings. Glue in place. Glue photos on frame centered in openings.*

6. Glue one frame on each side of inside of backing.

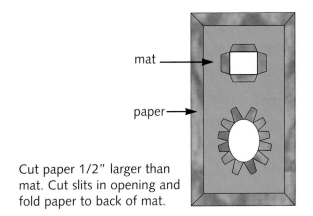

mat ———→

paper ———→

Cut paper 1/2" larger than mat. Cut slits in opening and fold paper to back of mat.

LAGUNA BEACH

Involving a child in creating scrapbook pages is an excellent way to have quality time together. Make a basic background scene, keeping it simple so the child will have plenty of room to create. Let them embellish the scene with stickers - any way they want to do it!

SUPPLIES

- Paper Pizazz: Orange, Yellow, Gold, Red (Plain Brights), Blue (Solid Jewel Tones), Sand (Handmade Paper), Cloud (Vacation)
- ZIG MS Markers: Orange Writer
- Border Buddy Jr.: Geometric
- Accu-Cut Dies: Sun
- Stickopotamus Stickers: Shore, Fish, Paradise
- Acid-free glue or XyronAdhesive Cartridge

Design by Jennie Dayley for Stickopotamus

INSTRUCTIONS

1. Using scallop edge of geometric Border Buddy, trace waves on blue paper and cut out. Cut mounds for beach from sand paper. Cut sun die-cut from yellow and gold paper. Glue sand, water and sun on cloud paper.
2. Cut mats for photos. Glue mats on page but not photos.
3. Let child attach stickers as they wish. Glue photos on mats. Print journaling with orange Writer.

Design by Jennie Dayley for Stickopotamus

SNOW FUN

SUPPLIES

- ❧ Paper Pizazz: Blue (Solid Muted Colors)
- ❧ White paper
- ❧ Fiskars: Deckle Paper Edgers
- ❧ ZIG MS Markers: White Fine Opaque Writer
- ❧ Stickopotamus Stickers: Winter Accessories
- ❧ Acid-free glue or Xyron Adhesive Cartridge

INSTRUCTIONS

1. Cut 1/4" off all sides of white paper. Glue on blue paper. Trim 1/2" off all sides of blue paper with Deckle edgers. Glue on white paper.

2. Print title with white Opaque Writer.

3. Cut mounds for snow hill from white paper. Glue

mounds on page. Let child attach stickers as they wish.

4. Cut mats for photos and trim with Deckle edgers. Glue mats on page but not photos.

5. Glue photos on mats. Print journaling and draw snowflakes with fine tip of white Opaque Writer.

KIDS IN THE STRAW

Design by Kate Stephani for Krause Publications

SUPPLIES

- Paper Pizazz: Brown Plaid (Great Outdoors), Orange, Gold (Plain Brights), 2 Browns, Green, Rust (Solid Jewel Tones)
- Black paper
- Fiskars: Paper Edgers - Scallop, Alligator, Arabian Nostalgia Corner Edgers Paper Crimper
- ZIG MS Markers: Black Writer
- Accu-Cut Dies: Pumpkin, Fence, Alphabet
- Templates: circle, oval
- Acid-free glue or Xyron Adhesive Cartridge

INSTRUCTIONS

1. Cut one brown paper and one brown plaid paper in half. Trim 1/4" off all sides of each paper. Glue one of each paper on two black papers, having borders even.
2. Crop photos, including one circle and one oval. Mat oval on gold, brown and rust paper. Trim each mat with Scallop edgers. Mat circle on gold, then rust. Trim each mat with Alligator edgers. Trim square photo on rust, then green. Trim each mat with Arabian edgers. Mat on gold paper. Cut corners of last photo with Nostalgia corner edgers. Mat on green, then gold paper. Cut across corners with Alligator edgers.
3. Cut letters from orange paper. Cut pumpkin from orange and gold paper. Cut fence from tan paper. Crimp pumpkins and fence. Glue gold behind orange pumpkin face and orange behind gold pumpkin face.
4. For journaling, cut large rectangle for title and small rectangles for kids' names. Mat large rectangle on green, then plaid paper.
5. Arrange all items on page and glue in place. Make dot and stitch line accents with black Writer.

PHOTO PUZZLES

SUPPLIES

- Twelve 1½" Woodsies squares
- Delta: Cherished Memories Paper Paint - two colors of choice
  Top Coat Satin Spray
- Ruler
- 1" sponge paintbrush
- Acid-free glue or Xyron Adhesive Cartridge

Design by Kate Stephani for Krause Publications

INSTRUCTIONS

Note: Puzzle can be two sided. Paint each side of squares different colors and glue a different photo on each side.

1. Paint each side of wood squares with at least two coats of paint. Let dry.

2. See step by step photos. Draw grid same size as number of squares used. Place photo in center of grid, having equal size border all around. Trim photo if needed. Tape photo in place with low-tack tape. Draw lines of grid on back of photo.

3. Cut photo apart. Glue photos on squares, being careful to position correctly according to where border should be. Spray puzzle with top coat satin spray. *Options: Use decoupage in place of spray; Laminate photos before gluing them on squares.*

Paint wood squares.

Draw grid to scale.

Draw grid on back of photo.

Cut photo pieces.

Glue photos on squares.

Spray with protective finish.

BATHING BEAUTIES

Design by Jennie Dayley for Stickopotamus

SUPPLIES

- Paper Pizazz: Yellow, Green, Pink, Blue (Plain Brights)
- White paper
- Fiskars: Scallop Paper Edgers
- ZIG MS Markers: White Fine Opaque Writer
  Fine & Chisel - Pink, Yellow
  Writers - colors of choice

- Stickopotamus Stickers: Mini-Flower, Paradise
- Oval template
- Acid-free glue or Xyron Adhesive Cartridge

INSTRUCTIONS

1. Ask child to draw picture of event you are about to record. Use colors in child's artwork throughout page.

2. For borders, cut four 3/4"-wide strips of green paper. Mat on pink paper. Glue on top and bottom of yellow paper. Alternate mini-flower stickers with white dots across center of border.

3. Crop one photo using oval template. Mat on blue paper. Trim with Scallop edgers. Mat other photo on pink, then blue paper. Cut rectangle for journaling and mat on blue paper. Print title with pink Fine & Chisel marker.

4. Glue child's artwork on one page. Glue photos and rectangle on other. Print journaling around photos with pink Fine marker. Add palm tree and flower stickers, overlapping one photo.

HULA HIPS

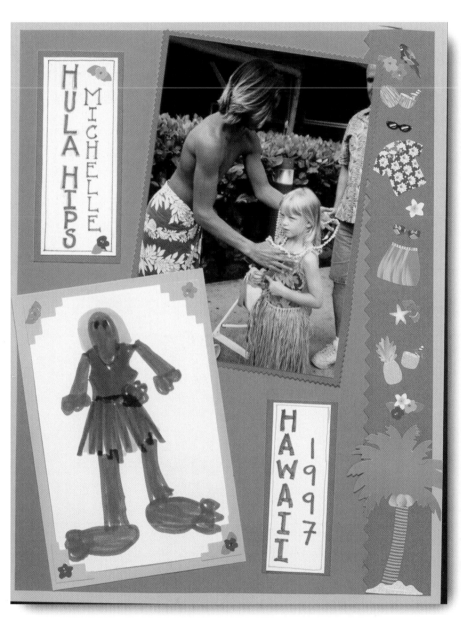

Design by Jennie Dayley for Stickopotamus

SUPPLIES

- Paper Pizazz: Turquoise, Yellow, Pink (Plain Brights)
- White paper
- ZIG MS Markers:
  Fine & Chisel - Pink, Yellow, Blue
  Writers - colors of choice
- Fiskars:
  Paper Edgers - Pinking, Stamp
  Art Deco Corner Edger
- Stickopotamus Stickers: Paradise
- Acid-free glue or Xyron Adhesive Cartridge

INSTRUCTIONS

1. Have child draw a picture of herself/himself on white paper. Mat on yellow paper. Cut four corners with Art Deco corner edgers. Glue corners on white paper. Place flower sticker on each corner.

2. Trim 1/4" off each side of turquoise paper and glue on yellow paper. Cut 1½" strip of pink paper and trim one edge with Pinking edgers. Glue strip vertically along one edge of turquoise paper. Adhere stickers along border that match theme of page.

3. Mat photo on pink paper and trim with Stamp paper edgers. Cut two rectangles from white paper for journaling. Mat on pink paper. Print journaling with pink and blue Fine & Chisel markers. Draw straight line around one rectangle with pink Fine marker and add stickers. Glue photo, artwork and rectangles on page.

CHAPTER 9

WEDDINGS

THREE-DIMENSIONAL ROSE FRAME

INSTRUCTIONS

See Stenciling General Instructions on page 19.

1. Place mat with rectangular opening on piece of parchment paper. With pencil, lightly trace around mat. Make second line 1/2" away from first.

2. Stencil parts of tea rose around frame drawn on parchment paper, letting leaves and buds go into center and off edge. Use art knife to carefully cut around leaves and buds that go into center, but don't cut beyond frame edge line.

3. Place stenciled paper face down on work surface. Glue along inside edges between leaves and buds.

4. Place mat on paper. Fold back glued tabs. Glue around outside edges of paper. Miter corners and fold paper over mat edges.

5. Tape photo in mat with arch opening. Tape arch mat in rectangular opening. Cover cardboard with parchment paper in same way as outside edge of frame. Glue cardboard on back of frame. Glue triangular easel on back of cardboard.

6. For three-dimensional flowers, stencil rosebuds on another piece of parchment paper. Cut petals apart. Attach 1/4" pieces of double-sided foam tape to backs of petals and position them over the stenciled petals on frame mat.

Design by Julie McGuffee for American Traditional Stencils

SUPPLIES

- American Traditional Stencil: CDS-3 Tea Rose
- 3 sheets 9" x 12" parchment paper
- 8" x 10" mat board (precut with rectangular opening or use art knife to cut opening)
- 5" x 7" mat (precut with arch opening or use art knife to cut opening)
- 8" x 10" cardboard
- Paints: mauve, yellow, green (colors of choice)
- Art knife
- 1/2" x 6" strips of double-sided 1/8" foam tape
- 1/4" stencil brush
- Tape, ruler, pencil
- Acid-free glue or Xyron Adhesive Cartridge

WEDDING ALBUM

Design by Jean Kievlan for Xyron

SUPPLIES

- ❧ Paper Pizazz: Metallic Gold (Metallic Papers), White Roses (Floral Papers), 2 Greens (Solid Muted Colors)
- ❧ Accu-Cut Dies: Champagne Glass, Wedding Rings, Mini Leaf
- ❧ White photo album
- ❧ Sheet protector
- ❧ White paper doilies: 4" heart, 6" round, 4" round
- ❧ 1/4"-wide gold metallic ribbon
- ❧ Acid-free glue or Xyron Adhesive Cartridge

INSTRUCTIONS

1. Glue lace doilies on album, overlapping to create pleasing design.

2. Laminate photos. *Option: Insert photos in sheet protector so each fits in one corner. Trim away sheet protector from remaining two sides to create pocket for photos.* Glue photos on album. Cut ribbon to fit along sides of photo pockets. Glue ribbons along edges of photo pockets, making sure ribbon seals pocket to surface of album.

3. Cut set of champagne glasses and gold rings from gold metallic paper. Cut 13 leaves from green papers. Cut nine rose motifs from floral paper. Glue roses and die-cuts on album.

GOLD WEDDING RINGS

Design by Julie McGuffee for Accu-Cut

SUPPLIES

- ❧ Paper Pizazz: White Roses (Floral Papers), Mauve, 2 Greens (Solid Muted Colors), Metallic Gold (Metalllic Papers)
- ❧ Fiskars: Victorian Paper Edgers
- ❧ Accu-Cut Dies: Wedding Rings, Mini Leaf
- ❧ Acid-free glue or Xyron Adhesive Cartridge

INSTRUCTIONS

1. Trim photos if needed. Mat on mauve paper and trim with Victorian edgers.

2. Cut rose motifs from paper. Cut green leaves and gold metallic wedding rings using die-cuts.

3. Arrange photos, roses and die-cuts on page. Glue in place.

EMBOSSED FRAME CARD & LAVENDER GIFT CARD

DRY EMBOSSED CARDS

SUPPLIES

- American Traditional Stencils: Brass or Blue Laser
- 65 lb. white paper
- Vellum
- Fiskars: Paper Edgers
- ZIG MS Pencils: Pastels
- Accu-Cut Dies: Card Template, Deckle Border, Oval
- 8" picot 1/4"-wide satin ribbon
- 1/8" circle punch
- Stylus
- Acid-free glue or Xyron Adhesive Cartridge

INSTRUCTIONS

Note: See Stenciling and Embossing General Instructions on pages 19-21.

Frame Card

1. Cut vellum and paper with card template. Trim vellum with Deckle edgers. Fold each piece in half and cut an oval on front of each card. Lay vellum face down on top of your chosen stencil design. The oval cutout (front of card) will be on your left.

2. Emboss design by tracing stencil pattern with stylus. Press firmly, using large end of stylus for bolder lines and smaller end for tiny design areas. *Option: After embossing is complete, lightly color backs of embossed areas with pencils.*

3. Glue vellum on paper card, making sure ovals are aligned. *Note: Glue vellum on front of card before back to maintain good fold line.* Punch two holes on folded edge. Insert ribbon and tie in bow. Cut ends at slant. Glue ribbon vertically along front edge of card. Glue photo in oval opening.

Gift Card

1. Cut paper with card template. Cut velum to fit front of card. Trim with Deckle edgers.
2. Emboss same as for frame card.

Designs by Julie McGuffee for American Traditional Stencils

JULIA & BRIAN

SUPPLIES

- Paper Pizazz: Pink, Lavender, Cream (Plain Pastels), Burgundy (Solid Jewel Tones)
- Fiskars:
  5" Micro-Tip Scissors
  Swivel Knife
  Circle Cutter
  Paper Edgers - Cotton Candy, Notch, Stamp, Cloud, Seagull
  McCall's Remember the Years™ 1950-1959 Papers
- ZIG MS Markers: Gold Opaque Writer, Burgundy Writer
- Lace motif & ribbon
- Oval template
- Pencil
- Acid-free glue or Xyron Adhesive Cartridge

Design by Fiskars, Inc.

INSTRUCTIONS

1. Crop photo in an oval. Vary width and decorative cut of each mat for very dramatic and lacy look. Mat photo on cream paper. Trim with Cotton Candy edgers, leaving 1/4" mat. Glue mat on burgundy paper and cut very close to first mat with same edgers. Glue mat on lavender paper and trim with Notch edgers. Glue mat on burgundy paper and trim with same paper edgers in reverse position. Glue mat on pink paper and trim with Stamp edgers. Glue mat on burgundy paper and trim with Cloud edgers. Draw line around outside edge of last mat with gold Opaque Writer. Add small dot accents.

2. Position matted photo on lacy paper and lightly mark where it overlaps background page design. With swivel knife, cut around marked area, making sure not to cut beyond it. Slide matted photo into slot and glue in place.

3. With circle cutter, cut 4" burgundy circle. Cut 3/4"-wide border. Trim outside edge with Cloud edgers. Glue ribbon and lace motif on circle. Draw gold accent line around circle with gold Opaque Writer. Draw gold and burgundy line around edge of border.

4. Write names of couple with gold Opaque Writer. Add burgundy accent lines.

INVITATION ENVELOPES

SUPPLIES

- Paper Pizazz: Flowers (Floral Papers)
- ZIG MS Markers: Fine Opaque Writer - Gold, Silver
- Fiskars: Paper Edgers - Imperial, Majestic
- Vellum paper
- Acid-free glue or Xyron Adhesive Cartridge

Designs by Carol Snyder for EK Success

INSTRUCTIONS

1. Cut vellum to size for addressing on front of envelope. Write address on vellum using gold or silver Opaque Writer.

2. PINK ENVELOPE: Cut vellum with Majestic edgers and mat on pink floral paper. Trim paper, leaving 1/2" border. Glue on envelope. WHITE ENVELOPE: Mat vellum on pink floral paper leaving 1/4" border. Draw wavy line around border with gold Opaque Writer. LAVENDER ENVELOPE: Cut pansy floral paper 1/4" and 1½" wide and length of vellum. Trim one edge of wider border with Imperial edgers. Glue borders along top and bottom edge of vellum.

3. Glue matted vellum on front of envelope.

HEART WEDDING BOOK

Design by Judy Barker for American Traditional Stencils

SUPPLIES

- American Traditional Stencils: BL-121 Heart Trims & Frame, MS-111 Calligraphy, MS-36 Numbers
- Fiskars: Victorian Paper Edgers
- Paints: colors of choice
- Stencil brush
- Art knife
- Light table or other light source
- Tape, ruler, sponge
- Acid-free glue or Xyron Adhesive Cartridge

INSTRUCTIONS

Note: See Stenciling and Embossing General Instructions on pages 19-21.

1. To sponge cover, mix one part paint to three parts water. Dip sponge in paint and squeeze out excess water. Tap surface lightly. For binder, cut 1" x 5½" strip of paper. Trim with Victorian edgers. Sponge on paint using less water for more intense color. Glue along fold of cover.

2. Cut four 5½" x 8½" pieces of cardstock. Fold in half to 4½" x 5½".

3. Emboss three cards on inside right page for picture frames. Cut out centers with art knife. Tape photos behind openings. Stencil cover with heart stencil.

4. To assemble, place photo frame cards inside cover. Glue along spine. Glue backside of each frame card to front of adjacent card.

MEREDITH

SUPPLIES

- Paper Pizazz: Pink, White, Cream, Peach (Plain Pastels), Pink Moire´, Laser Lace (Wedding)
- Fiskars: Arabian Paper Edgers
- ZIG MS Markers: Black Calligraphy, Black Writer
- Acid-free glue or Xyron Adhesive Cartridge

INSTRUCTIONS

1. Trim lace paper with Arabian edgers. Glue strip on each side of page.

2. Mat photo on pink paper and trim with same edgers. Mat on cream, then peach papers.

3. Glue matted photo on center of page. Cut a cream oval for journaling. Mat on pink, then cream paper. Use black Calligraphy marker to write name. Add designs with black Writer. Glue oval on page.

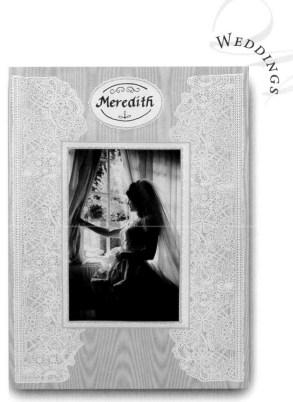

Design by LeNae Gerig for Hot Off The Press

TORN PAPER CARD

SUPPLIES

- American Traditional Stencil: GS-121 Rosewood Frame
- 4¼" x 5½" (folded) white card with matching envelope
- 4¼" x 5½" cranberry handmade paper
- 3½" x 2½" white cardstock
- Paints: red, green, brown, yellow (or colors of choice)
- 3/16" stencil brush
- Art knife
- Acid-free glue or Xyron Adhesive Cartridge

INSTRUCTIONS

Note: See Stenciling General Instructions on page 19.

1. Stencil rosewood frame on small piece of cardstock. Cut out inside opening and around outside border, leaving narrow white edge.

2. Moisten 1/4" border around handmade paper. Pull fibers to create feathered edge. Glue handmade paper on front of white card.

3. Glue photo on back of rosewood frame. Glue framed photo on center of card.

Design by Judy Barker for
American Traditional Stencils

STRING OF PEARLS

Design by Stacy Julian for Creating Keepsakes Magazine

SUPPLIES

- Paper Pizazz: Wedding Paper (satin)
- Paper: black, gray, white
- Fiskars: Paper Edgers - Provincial, Colonial, Scallop
- Acid-free glue or Xyron Adhesive Cartridge

INSTRUCTIONS

1. Trim 1/8" off all sides of black paper. Glue on gray paper.

2. Mat photos on white paper and trim with Provincial edgers. Glue on gray paper and trim with Colonial edgers.

3. For pearls, draw line on white paper in shape of strand of pearls. The strand is easier to cut if it isn't complete circle. Using Scallop edgers, cut along right side of drawn line. Turn paper around and cut back along strand being sure to match points of Scallop edgers across from each other to create look of pearls.

4. Arrange photo and pearls on page. Glue in place, tucking ends of pearls under photo.

THANK YOU CARD

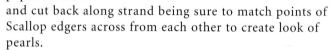

Design by Julie McGuffee for Accu-Cut

SUPPLIES

- Paper Pizazz: Laser Lace (Romantic Papers), Pretty Punch-Outs Border and Flowers
- Pale green cardstock
- Fiskars: Paper Edgers - Clouds, Deckle
- ZIG MS Markers: Fine Opaque Writers - White, Lilac Chisel Opaque Writer - White
- Accu-Cut Dies: Small Heart #3, Card Template, Oval Picture Frame
- 8" lilac 1/8"-wide satin ribbon
- 1/8" circle punch
- Acid-free glue or Xyron Adhesive Cartridge

INSTRUCTIONS

1. Cut card from cardstock with scalloped edge.

2. Cut frame and heart from white paper. Trim heart with Clouds edgers and frame with Deckle edgers. Punch two holes at top of heart. Insert ribbon through holes and tie in bow. Cut ends at a slant.

3. Glue laser lace across front of card. Glue flower punch-out on heart. Glue heart on center of laser lace. Add dots along top edge of paper lace and along scallop border with fine white Opaque Writer.

4. Glue photo in oval opening of frame. Glue frame on inside of card. Glue floral border along top and bottom edges of frame. Write "Thank You" with white chisel Opaque Writer. Add shadow and dots with fine lilac Opaque Writer. Make cluster of three dots randomly around card with white and pink Writers.

DAVENA AND GEORGE

Design by Katie Hacker for Hot Off The Press

SUPPLIES

- Paper Pizazz: Purple, White Flowers (Floral Papers), Ferns (Great Outdoors), Gold Metallic (Metallic Papers), Green (Solid Jewel Tones)
- Fiskars: Rounder Corner Edgers
- ZIG MS Markers: Black Calligraphy Writer, Black Writer
- Acid-free glue or Xyron Adhesive Cartridge

INSTRUCTIONS

1. Cut three 1/2"-wide gold metallic strips. Round corners of full sheet of green fern paper. Position strips horizontally behind fern paper and glue on 12" x 12" white floral paper.

2. Rounding all corners, mat photo on gold paper, then on wider purple flower paper. Mat on green, then gold paper.

3. Cut oval for journaling. Mat on green, then gold paper. Write caption with black Writer.

CHAPTER 10

NATURE & SCENERY

GRAM'S FLOWERS

Design by Jean Kievlan for Accu-Cut

SUPPLIES

❧ Paper Pizazz: Pink (Plain Pastels), lavender, pink, green, blue (Light Great Backgrounds), 2 greens (Solid Muted Colors), Yellow, Pink, Lavender, Turquoise (Plain Brights)

❧ ZIG MS Markers: Black Writer

❧ Accu-Cut Dies: Mini Butterfly, Mini Bee, Grass Border, Lower Case Collegiate (2")

❧ Flower sticker

❧ Acid-free glue or Xyron Adhesive Cartridge

INSTRUCTIONS

1. Cut butterflies, bee, grass border and letters from appropriate colored paper using dies. Note that butterflies are cut in half and two different colors are glued together. Arrange and glue photos and die-cuts on page.

2. Draw detail accents on die-cuts and journal using black Writer. Press flower sticker on grass.

POP-UP SPRING

Design by Julie McGuffee for Accu-Cut

SUPPLIES

- ❧ Paper Pizazz: Daisies (Romantic Paper), Pink, Green, Lavender, Yellow, Gold (Plain Pastels), 2 Greens (Solid Muted Colors)
- ❧ White cardstock
- ❧ Paper Edgers: Dragon Back
- ❧ ZIG MS Markers: Fine Opaque Writers - White, Yellow
- ❧ Accu-Cut Dies: Nested Flower, Mini Leaves, Small Oval, Mini Leaves, Cutwork Chevron Card, Small Tulip, Grass Border, Lower Case Traveler Alphabet
- ❧ Acid-free glue or Xyron Adhesive Cartridge

INSTRUCTIONS

Note: See Pop-Up and Pop-Around General Instructions on page 23.

1. Cut cutwork chevron card from white paper. Working from front of card, bend first, then every other "V" down, tucking points to back of card.

2. For nested flower chain, accordion fold pink paper lengthwise, then cut flower shape. Fold each flower in half again.

3. For tulip chain, fold dark green paper into quarters, then in half again to form triangle. Place on die with point toward bottom of tulip pattern and folded edges within outer pattern line. Cut to form tulip circle ("die-cut doily").

4. Cut two adjacent tulip shapes out of circle and set them aside for another project. Cut tulip flower heads from different colored papers and glue on tulip circle.

5. Glue grass border along bottom of inside of card.

6. Glue ends of nested flower chain to bottom inside of card about 1" from outer edges.

7. Glue two end tulips on left and two end tulips on right of card. Don't glue two center tulips. When card is folded, these two flowers will fold down inside and will pop up when card is opened. The flower chain across bottom will pop out too.

8. Glue letters of "Spring" across center of card. Embellish letters and tulips with white dots.

9. Cut photo in oval and mat on green paper. Trim mat with Dragonback edgers. Glue on front of card. Glue flower and two leaves on bottom of oval.

10. Cut daisy paper with edgers and glue on yellow paper.

11. Arrange and glue card and three flower die-cut shapes on page.

BRIAN AT THE LAKE HOUSE

SUPPLIES

- Paper Pizazz: Brown, Orange, Green (Solid Jewel Tones)
- ZIG MS Markers: Gold Fine Opaque Writer
- Fiskars: Deckle Paper Edgers
- Stickopotamus Stickers: Fall Leaves
- Acid-free glue or Xyron Adhesive Cartridge

INSTRUCTIONS

1. Cut two strips of brown paper 1¾" wide and trim with Deckle edgers. Cut two strips 1¼" wide and trim in same way. Glue narrow strips on wide strips. Press leaf stickers on center of each strip. Glue one strip across top of page and other along one side. Cut excess ends.

2. Triple mat photo with brown trimmed with edgers.

Design by Jennie Dayley for Stickopotamus

Mat on green and orange, leaving room for journaling on bottom of green mat. Journal and add accents with gold Opaque Writer.

LEAF WRAPPING PAPER

SUPPLIES

- Plain brown wrapping paper
- Delta: Cherished Memories Green paper paint
- 1" painting sponge
- Soft leaf
- Acid-free glue or Xyron Adhesive Cartridge

INSTRUCTIONS

1. Use sponge to apply thin layer of paint to underside of leaf.

2. Press leaf on brown paper. When dry, wrap package.
Options: Use different colors of paint and items such as thistles, wheat, or pine boughs.

Design by Deanna Lambson for Creating Keepsakes Magazine

RED FLOWERS

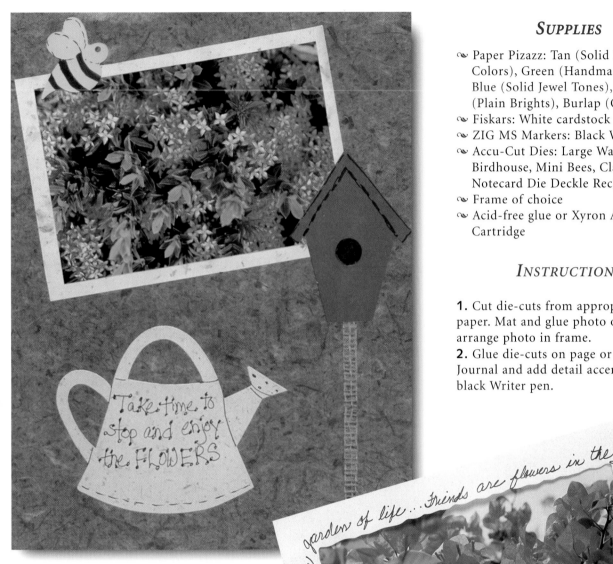

SUPPLIES

- ❧ Paper Pizazz: Tan (Solid Muted Colors), Green (Handmade Papers), Blue (Solid Jewel Tones), Yellow (Plain Brights), Burlap (Country)
- ❧ Fiskars: White cardstock
- ❧ ZIG MS Markers: Black Writer
- ❧ Accu-Cut Dies: Large Watering Can, Birdhouse, Mini Bees, Classic Notecard Die Deckle Rectangle
- ❧ Frame of choice
- ❧ Acid-free glue or Xyron Adhesive Cartridge

INSTRUCTIONS

1. Cut die-cuts from appropriate paper. Mat and glue photo on page or arrange photo in frame.
2. Glue die-cuts on page or photos. Journal and add detail accents using black Writer pen.

Designs by Jean Kievlan for Accu-Cut

COLORADO ROCKIES

Design by Julie McGuffee for Accu-Cut

SUPPLIES

- Paper Pizazz: Brown, Orange (Solid Muted Colors)
- Cardstock: black, tan
- Paper Edgers: Dragonback, Deckle
- ZIG MS Markers: Black Writer, Orange Extra Fine Opaque Writer
- Accu-Cut Dies: Tree/No Leaves, Small Oak Leaf
- Delta Paper Paint: yellow, tan, orange
- 1" flat paintbrush
- Foam sheet
- Acid-free glue or Xyron Adhesive Cartridge

INSTRUCTIONS

1. Mat photos on brown paper and trim with Deckle edgers.

2. Make small birch leaf stamp by cutting shape from foam. Dip foam shape in paint and press on tan paper. Use three different colors, overlapping leaves. When dry, glue photos on page.

3. Cut one tree die-cut from brown paper and one from black paper. Glue together, slightly offset. Silhouette photo and glue on page. Glue tree on page, slightly overlapping photo.

4. Cut small birch leaf die-cut and glue on page for journaling. Journal and add detail accents using black Writer. Add orange highlights on letters with Opaque Writer.

ALASKA

Design by Julie Stephani for Krause Publications

SUPPLIES

- Paper Pizazz: Trees (Vacation), Green, Brown (Solid Muted Colors), Blue, Yellow, Green, Tan (Plain Pastels), Punch Outs - Tree, Cabin, Bear (Outdoors)
- White cardstock
- Fiskars: Peaks Paper Edgers, Circle Paper Cutter, Circle Punch
- ZIG MS
  Markers: Black Writer
  Yellow Opaque Writer
- Acid-free glue or Xyron Adhesive Cartridge

INSTRUCTIONS

Note: See Envelope General Instructions on page 14.

1. Crop and single or double mat photos. Crop several photos with circle cutter and trim with Peaks edgers. Arrange photos on two pages, overlapping when possible. Have one photo go across both pages, cutting it along edge of pages.

2. For more detailed journaling, number photos and journal on separate sheet of paper. Punch yellow circles for numbers and glue close to each photo. Type title and cut into rectangle. Double mat rectangle and glue on page.

3. Make envelope to store journaling. Fold 8" x 11" paper in thirds. Cut flap in a point with Peaks edgers. Outline envelope in stitches with yellow Opaque Writer. Glue punch-outs on front of envelope. Type title and cut into rectangle. Double mat rectangle and glue on envelope. Draw stitch accents with black Writer.

CHAPTER 11

SCHOOL

SCHOOL DAYS BOX

Design by Heidi Geffen for Sticker Planet

SUPPLIES

- Sticker Planet: The Gifted Line Stickers - Vacation, School Days
  Sandylion Stickers
- Charms or trinkets
- Acid-free glue or Xyron Adhesive Cartridge

INSTRUCTIONS

Recycle an old box into a new treasure! If decorating a cigar box, strategically place the stickers over the logo or words. Areas of the box can be covered with solid colored sticker paper before applying individual designs. The fun continues when you open the box. Try creating a sticker border along the inside to match the design within. Add charms or trinkets.

FIRST DAY OF SCHOOL

SUPPLIES

- Paper Pizazz: Yellow, Red (Plain Brights)
- Cardstock: black, white
- ZIG MS Markers: Opaque Extra-Fine White, Black Writer
- Mrs. Grossman's Stickers: Black and White Border, Red and White Border, School Border, Vehicles, School, Classroom Stuff, Apple, Pens and Crayons
- Sticker Planet Pop-Dots
- Oval Template
- Acid-free glue or Xyron Adhesive Cartridge

Design by Heidi Geffen for Sticker Planet

INSTRUCTIONS

1. Choose three basic colors and use them throughout as shown with black, yellow and red. For border, use one strip each from three borders listed above. Start along outer edge and work in, one color at a time.

2. For each frame, cut 4½" x 6¼" piece from white cardstock. Use oval template to crop photo. Mat photo with thin border of yellow or red. Adhere stickers all around card. Stickers that go off the sides can be cut along edge and remaining piece can be used on mat. For dimension, press a Pop-Dot on one sticker and place another sticker of same design on top of it.

3. Mat frames with yellow and red, then again on black leaving extra paper on one end for journaling. Use white marker to print on black paper for chalkboard look.

4. Print title and embellish with stickers.

MARTY

SUPPLIES

- Paper Pizazz: Red Plaid, Yellow, Ruled (Our School Days), Blue (Solid Muted Colors), School Punch-Outs
- ZIG MS Markers: Black Writer
- Oval template
- Acid-free glue or Xyron Adhesive Cartridge

Design by Katie Hacker for Hot Off The Press

INSTRUCTIONS

1. Mat large school photo on patterned, then plain paper. Cut some photos in ovals. Mat other photos using patterned and complementary plain papers. Mat punch-outs for added emphasis.

2. Cut square sheet of yellow ruled paper for journaling. Print title with black Writer. Glue photos, punch-outs and journaling square on page.

LITTLE RED SCHOOL HOUSE

SUPPLIES

- Paper Pizazz: Kid's Drawing (School Days), Yellow, Red, Green (Plain Brights), Red, Brown (Solid Jewel Tones)
- White paper
- Fiskars: Paper Edgers - Jigsaw, Wave
    - 5" Micro-Tip Scissors
    - 45mm Rotary Cutter (wave and straight blades)
    - Cutting Mat
    - Paper Crimper
- ZIG MS Markers: Writers - Black, Red
- Accu-Cut Dies: Pencil, Apple
- Stickers: plane, hearts
- Pencil, ruler, black thread, brad
- Acid-free glue or Xyron Adhesive Cartridge

Design by Fiskars, Inc.

INSTRUCTIONS

1. Draw and cut out schoolhouse pattern. Trace all pieces except roof on red paper. Trace roof pattern on brown paper folded once, placing top of roof on fold. Trim bottom edges of roof with Wave edgers. Cut out pieces and run through crimper. Crimp roof again in opposite direction.

2. For journaling, trace roof on two sheets of white paper and cut out all three layers simultaneously with rotary cutter. Fold in half.

3. Cut two 1/8"-wide strips from red paper for windowpanes. Glue across window open-ing. Position and glue one photo behind widow and one behind door. Glue bell tower on green paper. Trim with Zipper edgers.

4. Glue all schoolhouse pieces on background paper. Glue gold brad on door.

5. Cut rectangle for journaling from white paper using Wave rotary cutter blade. Mat on red paper. Crimp and glue on page. Print title on yellow pencil die-cut with red Writer and glue on rectangle. Adhere plane sticker on red paper and cut around it in shape of a cloud. Glue on page. Cut two threads and glue ends under plane and journaling rectangle. Print journaling on red apple die-cut and glue on page.

TEACHER GIFT BOOK

SCHOOL

Designs by Toni Nelson for EK Success

SUPPLIES

- Paper Pizazz: Red, Green, Yellow, Blue, Striped, Cork (School Days)
- Border Buddy Jr.: Stars and Stripes, Geometric
- White cardstock
- 6½" x 8½" protective sheets
- Fiskars: Paper Edgers - Mini Scallop
    Swivel Knife
    Circle Cutter

- ZIG MS Markers:
    Writers - Red, Blue, Yellow, Green, Baby Blue, Violet
    Calligraphy Writer - Baby Blue
    Fine & Chisel - Violet, Green
- Stickopotamus Stickers: Classroom, Push Pins
- 1/8"-wide satin ribbon - red, blue
- Acid-free glue or Xyron Adhesive Cartridge

INSTRUCTIONS

1. Look what fun you can have making a mini album for a favorite teacher! Mat photos on brightly colored plain or patterned papers.
2. Make borders using templates and markers. Decorate pages with sticker accents.
3. Cut rectangles for journaling and mat them or write right on page with colorful Writers.
4. Tie pages together by inserting ribbons through precut holes. Tie ribbons in bows.

CONGRATS FRAME

SUPPLIES

- American Traditional Stencils: BL-477 Oval Cameo Frame, BL-491 Greetings, BL-88 Alphabet
- 8½" x 11" cardstock (color of choice)
- 8" cardboard easel (or make one from 8½" x 3½" cardboard)
- 8½" x 11" cardboard
- 3/16" stencil brush
- Paint (color of choice)
- Stylus
- Art knife
- Tape
- Acid-free glue or Xyron Adhesive Cardstock

Design by Judy Barker for American Traditional Stencils

INSTRUCTIONS

Note: See Stenciling and Embossing General Instructions on pages 19-21.

1. Center oval stencil on cardstock. Emboss with stylus. Stencil frame and ribbon. Stencil "Congratulations" and year. Drybrush light tint of color around outside edges of cardstock.

2. Use art knife to cut out inner oval opening.

3. Position photo in opening and tape in place. Glue cardboard on back of cardstock. Glue easel on back of cardboard.

Design by Fiskars, Inc.

SCHOOL DAYS

SUPPLIES

- Paper Pizazz: Pink, Blue (Plain Pastels)
- Black paper
- Fiskars: Spindle Paper Edgers,
      Rounder Corner Edgers
      5" Micro-Tip Scissors
      McCall's Remember the Years™ 1950-1959 Paper
- Boomerang template
- Pencil
- Acid-free glue or Xyron Adhesive Cartridge

INSTRUCTIONS

1. Crop photo corners with Rounder corner edgers. Glue on pink, black and blue paper trimmed with Spindle edgers. Glue on black paper and trim corners with Rounder corner edgers. Glue photo on page.

2. Type or print journaling on pink and blue paper.

Cut out using the boomerang template. Glue on black paper trimmed with Spindle edgers. Glue pink boomerang on blue and blue boomerang on pink paper. Trim with same edgers. Glue both on black paper and trim with same edgers. Glue boomerangs on page.

ABOUT ME

SUPPLIES

- Paper Pizazz: Tie-Dye (Teen Years), Yellow, Blue, Green, Pink, Purple (Plain Brights), Teen Years Cutouts
- Fiskars: Paper Edgers - Peaks, Ripple, Seagull
- ZIG MS Markers: Black Writer
- Templates: oval, circle, wavy heart
- Acid-free glue or Xyron Adhesive Cartridge

INSTRUCTIONS

1. Trim 1/2" off each side of tie-dyed paper and glue on purple paper.

2. Trim photos in various shapes using templates. Silhouette one photo. Trim with Peaks, Ripple or Seagull edgers. Glue photos on brightly colored papers.

3. Mat cutouts and fill in information with black Writer. Add dot and line accents on mats.

Design by LeNae Gerig for Hot Off The Press

GROOVE ON!

SUPPLIES

- Paper Pizazz: Tie-Dyed (50s & 60s), Green, Gold, Orange (Plain Brights)
- Fiskars: Bowtie Paper Edgers
- ZIG MS Markers: Black Writer
- Letter stickers
- Templates: circle, oval
- Acid-free glue or Xyron Adhesive Cartridge

INSTRUCTIONS

1. Create shirt design from tie-dyed paper. Draw accents with black Writer. Glue shirt on orange paper.

2. Use template to crop photos. Glue on bright paper and trim with Bowtie edgers. Glue photos on shirt. Glue letter stickers on shirt.

3. Cut blue square for journaling. Print title with black Writer. Add dot and line accents on top and bottom of square and page.

Design by Katie Hacker for Hot Off The Press

CHAPTER 12

CELEBRATIONS

MOM IS 80!

SUPPLIES

- ❧ Paper Pizazz: Torn Paper (Inspirations & Celebrations), Pink, Purple (Solid Jewel Tones)
- ❧ Fiskars: Deckle Paper Edgers
- ❧ ZIG MS Markers: Black Writer, Gold Opaque Writer
- ❧ Oval template
- ❧ Acid-free glue or Xyron Adhesive Cartridge

Design by Becky Goughnour for Hot Off The Press

INSTRUCTIONS

1. Choose close-up photo that includes honored guest and her gifts. Choose another photo that includes guests. Use oval template to trim photos and mat on purple and pink paper trimmed with Deckle edgers.

2. Glue photos around printed sentiment.
3. Cut rectangle for journaling and print letters with black Writer. Highlight with gold Writer.

TEA PARTY

INSTRUCTIONS

Cut the following pieces from cardstock:
5½" x 8½" – Menu, Invitation
3" x 3¾" – Name Card/Gift Tag
3" x 3¼" – Place Card

Menu/Invitation

1. Trace mini scallop border around each piece with Chisel tip.

2. Edge menu and invitation with broad tip of Calligraphy pen.

3. Connect border and edge with fine lines and dots.

4. Create flowers with corner circles. Doodle flower details, using fine tip for flowers and brush tip for leaves.

5. Print messages and names. Add flower accents.

Name Card/Gift Tag

1. Trace mini scallop border around name card. Cut out around bordered edge.

2. Draw inside edge and connect with fine lines and dots. Finish same as for Menu/Invitation.

Place Card

1. Fold piece along one edge so card will stand. Fold under 1" so front of card measures 2" x 3¼".

2. Trace mini scallop border across top and bottom. Edge card with broad Chisel tip. Connect border and edge with fine lines and dots. Finish same as for Menu/Invitation.

Designs by Toni Nelson and Beth Reames for EK Success

SUPPLIES

- Border Buddy Jr.: Geometric
- White cardstock
- ZIG MS Markers:
  Fine & Chisel - Spring Green, Hyacinth
  Writers - Baby Pink, Hyacinth, Violet, Pink
  Scroll & Brush - Green
  Calligraphy - Spring Green
- Acid-free glue or Xyron Adhesive Cartridge

FIRST BIRTHDAY

Jacob William
August 10, 1997

Design by Julie Stephani for Krause Publications

SUPPLIES

- Paper Pizazz: Striped (Birthday), Red, Green, Yellow, (Plain Brights), Punch-Out (Birthday)
- Fiskars Paper Edgers: Ripple
- ZIG MS Markers: Black Writer
- Accu-Cut Dies: Small Banner
- Acid-free glue or Xyron Adhesive Cartridge

INSTRUCTIONS

1. Cut striped paper with Ripple edgers. Glue onto green paper.

2. Mat photo on yellow, then red paper. Trim red mat with Ripple edgers. Glue mat on green paper and trim with straight edge. Remove photo from mat until strips are in place.

3. Cut red, green and yellow strips of paper a scant 1/4" wide. Arrange strips on page, weaving them together where they overlap. Glue on page.

4. Cut green rectangle for journaling. Mat on yellow paper and trim with edgers. Arrange rectangle and photo on page and glue down. Glue punch out on rectangle.

5. Cut banner die-cut from three colors of paper and glue together, overlapping them slightly. Glue on page. Add journaling with black Writer.

Designs by Beth Reames for EK Success

GEO PARTY

SUPPLIES

- Border Buddy Jr.: Geometric
- White cardstock
- Fiskars: Alligator Paper Edgers
- ZIG MS Markers: Writers - Green, Red, Blue, Yellow
  Calligraphy - Red
  Fine & Chisel - Blue
- Acid-free glue or Xyron Adhesive Cartridge

INSTRUCTIONS

Invitation and Place Mat
1. For each invitation, cut 4½" x 8½" piece from cardstock. For each place mat, use 8½" x 11" piece of cardstock. Trace mini zigzag border with Border Buddy bullet tip.

2. Draw geometric shapes in two corners. Draw straight lines around other two corners.

3. Print name or message. Make small dot accents. Draw colored edge border with broad tip of Calligraphy pen.

4. Write invitation information on inside of card. Laminate each place mat.

Thank You Card
1. Create two "geo" corners by overlapping circle, square and triangle corners.

2. Connect corners with straight lines using Chisel tip.

3. Print message. Make small dot accents. Draw colored edge border with broad tip of Calligraphy pen.

Treat Bag Tag
1. Create "geo" line by overlapping circle, square and triangle corner across top and bottom.

2. Print message. Make small dot accents. Draw colored edge border with broad tip of Calligraphy pen.

Gift Tag
1. Cut 2½" square from cardstock. Draw small geometric shapes on tag.

2. Draw stitch marks around outside edge. Print message.

3. Cut front bottom edge with Alligator edgers. Draw colored edge border with broad tip of Calligraphy pen along inside bottom edge. Punch hole in upper left corner. Attach string through holes with larkshead knot. Tape or tie strings on package.

CAITLIN'S BIRTHDAY

SUPPLIES

- Paper Pizazz: Fuchsia (Plain Brights) Lavender, Blue (Plain Pastels)
- Fiskars: Seagull Paper Edgers
    Nostalgia Corner Edgers
    Micro-Tip Scissors
    Paper Trimmer
    Basics II Stencil
- ZIG MS Markers: Black Writer
- Acid-free glue or Xyron Adhesive Cartridge

INSTRUCTIONS

1. Cut all four corners of two photos with Victorian corner edgers. Mat photos on lavender paper. Trim paper, leaving 1/4" mat. Trim corners of paper with same corner edgers.
2. Cut one 2" x 2" and one 2" x 2½" rectangle for journaling.

Design by Fiskars, Inc.

3. For ribbon strips, cut paper strips using parallel cuts with Seagull edgers. Position strips on matted photos and journal boxes and glue in place. For bows, cut small pieces of strips and glue on ribbons.
4. Crop two photos using "Word Cloud" stencil. Mat photos on pastel lavender paper trimmed with Seagull edgers. Add journaling.

IT'S MY BIRTHDAY!

SUPPLIES

- Paper Pizazz: Birthday (Quick & Easy Memory Mats)
- ZIG MS Markers: Black Writer
- Acid-free glue or Xyron Adhesive Cartridge

INSTRUCTIONS

Some papers come with mats built right into the page. What could be simpler? Cut out openings in paper. Choose photos to fit the mat openings and glue them to the back of paper. Journal "It's My Birthday!" on the mat to complete this easy page.

Design by LeNae Gerig for Hot Off The Press

ANNA BUNYAN

In the Headlines In 1898
- U.S. yearly automobile production reached 1,000.
- Radium, the first radio active element, was discovered.
- U.S. college football upped its touchdown point value from 4 to 5.
- The NY Times dropped in price from 3 cents to 1 cent.
- Milk cost 13 cents for a half gallon, delivered.
- Flour cost 14 cents for a 5 lb. bag
- 10 lbs. of potatoes cost 16 cents.
- The Rosary was the most popular song.
- The Turn of the Screw by Henry James and the War of the Worlds by H. G. Wells were published.
- "Hopalong Cassidy" was born.

celebrating 100 with my friend Anna Bunyan March 21, 1997

the MILLION DOLLAR question

On the morning of March 21, I boarded a Delta flight heading straight for Eugene Oregon. I left a beautiful spring day behind in SLC, and was a little disappointed when a very wet, dreary day greeted me in Oregon. I looked like a drowned rat at the party.

Q: How would Anna ever blow out 100 candles?

A: This was easily solved when several of her great grandsons showed up to help.

Design by Lisa Bearnson for Creating Keepsakes Magazine

SUPPLIES

- Paper Pizazz: Cocoa, Brown, Blue, Yellow (Solid Muted)
- Paper: white, yellow
- ZIG MS Markers: Black Millennium, Memory Pencils
- Fiskars: Heart Punch
- Acid-free glue or Xyron Adhesive Cartridge

INSTRUCTIONS

When someone celebrates a birthday that is a real milestone - like being 100 years old - it deserves special attention. Besides capturing photos on the page, have some fun! The candles across the bottom of the page fit in with the million dollar question, "How would Anna ever blow out 100 candles?" The answer is captured in a photo and journaling. Listing the headlines of what happened in 1898 adds a historical interest of what things were like the year Anna was born - as well as how much things have changed in those 100 years.

CHAPTER 13

MEMORY GIFTS

PHOTO BLOCKS

Design by Judy Barker for American Traditional Stencils

SUPPLIES

- American Traditional Stencils: BL-62 Stars, Hearts & Dots, BL-113 Fun Critters, BL-121 Heart Trims, BL-122 Cameo Trims, BL-134 Doodles, FS-946 Bouncing Baby
- 1" wooden blocks
- Acrylic paints of choice: white, red, blue, green, yellow
- 1" foam brush or sponge
- 1/4" stencil brush
- Clear sealer
- Acid-free glue or Xyron Adhesive Cartridge

INSTRUCTIONS

Note: See Stenciling General Instructions on page 19.
1. Use foam brush to paint wooden blocks. Mix paint colors is desired.
2. Position stencil on block, one side at a time. Mask around stencil to block out elements not used. Stencil in white. Allow to dry, then stencil again in color.
3. Stencil words and date first, then continue with images.

4. Use heart stencil and trace around photos. Cut out and glue to blocks. Some photos work better with block size than others. Trace block onto photo and cut.
5. Add stencil designs where desired. Tint edges with darker shade to antique. Allow to dry overnight and apply clear sealer.
Optional: To make blocks into Christmas ornaments, glue on ribbon.

STICKER FRAMES

Designs by Heidi Geffen for Sticker Planet

SUPPLIES

- EK Success: Maple Lane Press Frames
- Delta: Ceramcoat acrylic paint, Top Coat Satin spray
- The Gifted Line Stickers: Vacation, School, Animal

Antics, Flowers and Fruit, Victorian Charms, Fruit Harvest, Spring Flowers, Fancy Hat Cats, Toys
- Acid-free glue or Xyron Adhesive Cartridge

INSTRUCTIONS

Picture this! These frames are simple to create and make wonderful gifts. Decoupage simple wooden frames and layer them with an assortment of stickers. Or paint wood or canvas frames first, then add sticker designs.

Try cutting the stickers apart while they're still on the protective backing sheet. Then you can work with their placement before sticking them down. Finish the frame by spraying with a protective sealer.

ICELAND

Design by Mary Lee Burton for Creating Keepsakes Magazine

SUPPLIES

- Old World papers
- Paper: cream, brown
- Fiskars: Deckle Edge, Ripple Edge Scissors
- Snowflake paper punch
- Acid-free glue or Xyron Adhesive Cartridge

INSTRUCTIONS

1. Glue photos on cream paper. Trim with Deckle edgers. Glue on brown paper. Glue photos on page.
2. Type label and cut out. Glue on page. Stencil title and glue memorabilia on page. Punch snowflakes from brown paper and glue on page.

FREDA & NORRIS BOOK

Design by Julie McGuffee for Accu-Cut

SUPPLIES

- Paper Pizazz: Metallic Gold (Metallic Papers)
- Cardstock: burgundy, beige
- Fiskars: Victorian Paper Edgers
- ZIG MS Markers: Fine & Chisel Opaque Writer - Copper Penny
- Accu-Cut Dies: Border #110, Oval
- 2 Classic Ready to Make Frames
- 18" ecru 1/4"-wide satin ribbon
- Acid-free glue or Xyron Adhesive Cartridge

INSTRUCTIONS

1. Cut 16 (two per side) decorative strips from beige cardstock using the border die. Intertwine two strips and glue on front of frame.

2. Stack two frames on top of each other with openings facing and both hang tabs to right. Color outside edges of frames with copper Chisel Writer. Insert ribbon through holes of hang tabs.

3. Trim burgundy paper lengthwise, same width as frame. Cut remaining piece in half. For spine of book,
glue narrow piece along left side of back of one frame. While holding frames together, fold it around edges of both frames and glue on back of second frame. Glue remaining pieces of burgundy paper on backs of frame, overlapping spine.

4. Glue cream oval on gold paper. Trim 1/4" from edge with Victorian edgers. Glue on front of book.

Print names on oval with fine Opaque Writer and add dots around outside edge.

VICTORIAN KEEPSAKE FRAME

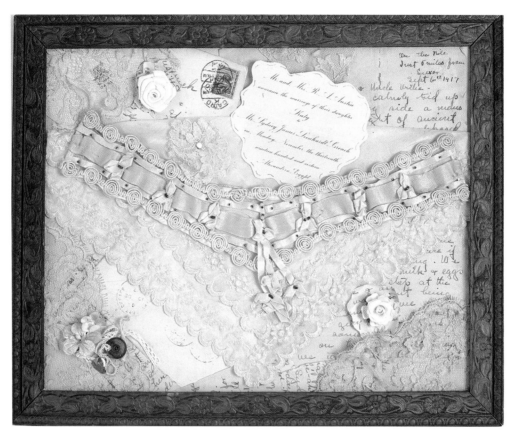

Design by Kathy Peterson for Krause Publications

SUPPLIES

- 13" x 16" vintage frame
- Vintage buttons, lace, flowers, love letters, stamped envelopes, hankie, trinkets, jewelry, wedding invitation
- Acid-free cardboard or foam board
- Acid-free brown paper
- Scissors, ruler, craft knife, frame tacks, picture hanger
- Acid-free glue or Xyron Adhesive Cartridge

INSTRUCTIONS

1. Using ruler and craft knife, cut piece of cardboard backing to frame.

2. Arrange vintage paper materials (except invitation) on backing and glue in place. Overlap paper pieces and fill in gaps with scraps of lace.

3. Fold the hankie in half in triangle shape and glue on center of design. Overlap hankie with lace pieces and wedding invitation. Cut invitation in abstract heart shape and draw broken wavy lines along edges.

4. Glue on buttons, scrap lace, flowers and jewelry to further embellish project. Trim off or fold under any pieces that overlap outside edges of backing and glue if necessary.

5. Attach keepsakes to frame with glue or frame tacks.

6. Glue brown paper to back of frame. Trim off excess with craft knife.

7. Attach frame hanger or display on easel.

ANGEL MEMORY ALBUM

Design by Susan Schultz for Krause Publications

SUPPLIES

- Walnut Hollow: Nostalgic Memory Album Cover #3702
- Delta: Ceramcoat - Light Ivory Acrylic Paint, Water Base Sealer, Renaissance Foil Adhesive and Gold Foil
- 5" x 7" angel card
- 2 yards 3"-wide flat ivory lace
- 2 yards 3/4"-wide flat ivory lace
- 2 yards 7/8"-wide ivory ribbon with wired gold edge
- Robert Simmons: 1" flat paintbrush
- Floral Pro glue gun
- Tack cloth, light sand-paper, paper towels
- Acid-free glue or Xyron Adhesive Cartridge

INSTRUCTIONS

1. Remove rivets from album and lightly sand front and back. Use tack cloth to remove dust. Apply light coat of sealer to all sides and let dry. Lightly sand and wipe again.

2. Apply two coats light ivory paint to front and back of album covers. Let dry between coats.

3. Starting at bottom left corner of album front, glue 3"-wide lace across bottom to other corner. Make mitered corner by lifting inside edge of lace to form 45 degree angle and continue gluing along next edge. Continue working around all edges of album, mitering each corner. Glue corners down flat.

4. Trim angel card to fit album. Glue trimmed card in center of album and glue 3/4" lace around card, overlap-ping edge of card 1/4" and mitering corners. Glue 7/8" lace along left edge of album, trimming lace along cor-ner edges.

5. Brush one coat foil adhesive on all lace. Let dry about 20 minutes and brush on another coat. Let dry at least one hour. The lace will be sticky. Cut 8" piece of gold foil and press dull side down on lace. Rub fingers over top of foil, lifting and moving foil to another area until all sticky areas are covered.

6. Apply two coats sealer to front and back of album. Let dry.

7. Tie bow in center of ribbon and glue bow 1½" above card. Twist and loop ribbon around album, gluing down about every inch. At center bottom, overlap ribbon ends 2" and cut ends in "V" shape. Fold ends back 1½".

FLAG GIFT BOX

Design by Carol Snyder for EK Success

SUPPLIES

- ❧ ZIG MS Markers:
    Woodcraft - Red, White, Blue
- ❧ Paper mache star box
- ❧ Flag picture or pattern
- ❧ Tracing paper and carbon paper
- ❧ Acid-free glue or Xyron Adhesive Cartridge

INSTRUCTIONS

1. Draw flag pattern and trace on lid of box using carbon paper.

2. Paint flag on box with Woodcraft markers. Blend colors for dimension.

3. Paint plaid band around side of box. *Option: Glue ribbon around box.* Outline and detail picture.

A STAR IS BORN GIFT BOX

SUPPLIES

- ❧ Paper Pizazz: Baby Prints (Baby)
- ❧ ZIG MS Markers: Steel Gray Writer
- ❧ Paper mache star box
- ❧ Tracing paper and carbon paper
- ❧ Star template
- ❧ Acid-free glue or Xyron Adhesive Cartridge

INSTRUCTIONS

1. Trace shape of box top on scrap of paper to make pattern. Divide points of stars into individual pieces and cut each out of coordinating papers. Trace and cut out star using template. Cut star from coordinating paper.

2. Glue all pieces on top of lid. Add lettering and doodle/detail line with gray Writer.

3. Cut band of coordinating paper for around side of box (3/4"-wide for box, 1/8"-wide for lid). Glue on bands, overlapping ends. Draw stitch lines above and below bands

*Design by
Carol Snyder for
EK Success*

TOOTH FAIRY GIFT BOX

SUPPLIES

- ❧ ZIG MS Markers:
  Fine Opaque Writers - Red, Green, Anniversary Ivory
  Extra-Fine Writer - Black
- ❧ Round wooden box
- ❧ Acid-free glue or Xyron Adhesive Cartridge

INSTRUCTIONS

1. Draw tooth on top of lid and color in with ivory Opaque Writer. Print "My Tooth Box" around box with red Opaque Writer. Add details with black writer.

2. Draw and color alternating squares and hearts around sides of box and lid.

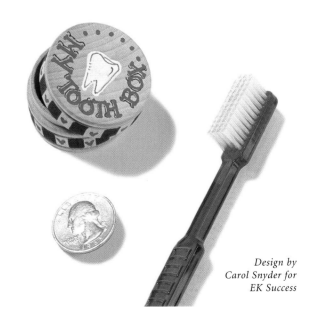

*Design by
Carol Snyder for
EK Success*

CHAPTER 14

MORE THAN ALBUMS

MEMORY WREATH

*Design by Billie Worrell for
Krause Publications*

SUPPLIES

- Delta: Archival Glue, Cherished Memories paper paints - Cherished Gold, Simply Sage, Cheeky Peach
- 3 corruboard frames (1 oval, 2 rectangles)
- Eucalyptus wreath
- Dried flowers and foliage
- 3" x 4" color photocopies of favorite photos
- #12 flat paintbrush
- Acid-free glue or Xyron Adhesive Cartridge

INSTRUCTIONS

1. Paint each frame a different color. Paint edges and backs of backing sheets, leaving one side unpainted.
2. Crop and glue photos on unpainted side of backing sheets. Glue frames on backs of backing sheets.
3. Arrange photos in wreath and glue in place. Glue sprigs of foliage and small flowers on tops of frames.

HEIRLOOM TABLE

Design by Julie Stephani for Krause Publications

SUPPLIES

- ❧ Paper Pizazz: Tapestry (Pretty Papers), Letters, (Black & White Photos), Burgundy, (Solid Jewel Tones), Cream, Blue (Plain Pastels)
- ❧ Black cardstock
- ❧ Fiskars: Paper Edgers - Victorian, Arabian Corner Edgers - Nostalgia
- ❧ Oval template
- ❧ 8" diameter lace circle

- ❧ Ribbon: 16" length 1/2"-wide floral satin wire-edged 4 yards 1/4"-wide mauve satin picot
- ❧ Two 3/4" mauve satin roses
- ❧ Mrs. Grossman's Stickers: Dove
- ❧ One 20" diameter round wooden table
- ❧ One 20" diameter round glass top
- ❧ One round tablecloth
- ❧ One lace table topper
- ❧ Acid-free glue or Xyron Adhesive Cartridge

INSTRUCTIONS

1. Drape table with tablecloth. Weave 1/4" ribbon through lace table topper 3" from outer edge of table. Tie ribbon in bow. Cut ribbon ends at a slant. Bow is center front of table.

2. Cut out around letters on patterned paper. Place in center of table. Crop and mat photos. Cut corners of one rectangular photo with Nostalgia corner edgers and mat on cream paper. Cut corners from burgundy paper and glue on corners of cream paper. Arrange photos on table.

3. Gather lace circle in center. Place gathered point under one photo. Tie floral ribbon in bow. Place satin roses on table. Place glass circle on top of table.

FRAMES

Designs by Jennie Dayley for Stickopotamus

SUPPLIES

General
- Classic Size Ready-to-Make frame
- Acid-free glue or Xyron Adhesive Cartridge

Jared
- ZIG MS Markers: Black Posterman Big & Broad Tip, Silver Fine Tip Opaque Writer
- Stickopotamus Stickers: Planets, Stars

Tub Time
- ZIG MS Markers: Light Blue Posterman Big & Broad Tip, Pink Chisel Tip Opaque Writer
- Stickopotamus Stickers: Bath Time

Alexis
- ZIG MS Markers: Yellow Posterman Big & Broad Tip, Pink Fine Tip Opaque Writer
- Stickopotamus Stickers: Makeup

Kimmie
- ZIG MS Markers: Pink Posterman Big & Broad Tip, Grape Juice Fine Tip Opaque Writer
- Stickopotamus Stickers: Makeup

Socks
- ZIG MS Markers: Green Posterman Big & Broad Tip, Black Writer
- Stickopotamus Stickers: Cat Accessories

INSTRUCTIONS

1. Paint frame with Big & Broad Tip marker.
2. Write name or title and decorate with Writer. Add stickers.

PHOTO MEMORY QUILT

Design by Julie Sowinski for Xyron

SUPPLIES

- ❧ White cotton fabric
- ❧ Photo transfer paper
- ❧ Quilt pattern of choice
- ❧ Acid-free glue or Xyron Adhesive Cartridge

INSTRUCTIONS

Note: See Photo Transfer General Instructions on page 17.

1. Select quilt pattern and determine size of photos needed.

2. Take photos and photo transfer paper to a copy shop to have color copies of photos made and printed on transfer paper. Reduce, enlarge or crop photocopies to fit quilt.

3. Transfer color copies to white fabric, following transfer instructions.

4. Run fabric through Xyron, using acid-free adhesive cartridge.

Note: Some fabrics have sizing, so run a small piece of fabric through the Xyron as a test. There should be a very fine even coat of adhesive on fabric. If sizing has repelled adhesive, wait a day to give adhesive time to absorb or wash fabric and run it through the Xyron again.

5. Pull away mask (clear cling plastic). If item is odd-shaped or has holes (such as lace), mask will remove adhesive from everywhere but fabric.

6. Cut pieces as desired. Save adhesive-backed scraps for use in gift bags, kids crafts or other quilts.

7. When ready to adhere, peel away white liner paper and position pieces. The adhesive allows you to pick up and reposition pieces.

8. If project won't require washing, stitching may not be necessary. If stitching item, avoid adhesive buildup on stitching needle by periodically running your fingers down needle. Once stitched, item can be washed or dry cleaned.

RIBBON
EMBROIDERY PILLOW

Design by Linda Wyszynski for Krause Publications
Stitches from Elegant Stitches by Judith Baker Montano

To secure ribbon to eye of needle, first thread needle with ribbon, then run needle through opposite end of ribbon 1/8" from end. Slide ribbon knot next to needle's eye. When making first stitch, leave 1/2" ribbon tail on backside of fabric. Push needle to right side. Gently pulling ribbon to front side, work first stitch and push needle to backside, piercing through ribbon tail on backside 1/4" from end of ribbon. When stitching is complete, push needle to back of fabric and run through ribbon on backside.

SUPPLIES

- 1/2 yard ecru tightly woven cotton fabric
- 1½ yards gathered 1¾"-wide crocheted lace
- 1 yard crocheted 1/2" flat lace
- 1 black and white 5" x 7" photo
- 1 sheet Photo Effects photo transfer paper
- Bucilla 4mm 100% Pure Silk Ribbon Embroidery:
  2 yards Banana (#502)
  1½ yards Light Hunter Green (#643)
  1½ yards Robin Egg Blue (#322)
  1 yard Pale Hunter Green (#633)
  24" Creamy Yellow (#655)
- Anchor Floss:
  1 yard Pale Peach Very Lt. (#366)
  24" Fern Green Very Lt. (#858)
- Chenille needle #20 (for floss and silk)
- Sharp sewing needle (to attach lace)
- 12" x 12" pillow form
- Sewing thread to match lace

INSTRUCTIONS

Note: If photo is larger than 5" x 7", increase amount of fabric and lace.

1. Follow directions on Photo Effects package to transfer photo to transfer paper

2. Transfer photo image to a 14" x 14" piece of cotton fabric. Let transfer dry for several hours.

3. Tack 1/2" lace around outside edge of photo with sewing thread. At corners, fold lace under, turn corner and fold under again. Folds should face each other to create flat pleat at edge of corner.

4. Refer to figures below and work flowers over lace. Use two strands of #366 floss to work spider rose bases, then finish roses with Banana silk. Work leaves with lazy daisy stitches in Light Hunter Green silk. Use four strands of #858 floss and stem stitch to work stems of Forget-Me-Nots. Use Robin Egg Blue silk for French knots and Creamy Yellow silk French knots for centers. Do leaves in Pale Hunter Green silk and straight stitch. Leave this stitch a little loose to create a puffy look.

5. Finish pillow, sewing double ruffle on outside edge. Using cotton fabric, make 2½" gathered ruffle with 1/2" seam allowance. Place 1½" gathered crocheted lace on top. Use 14" x 14" piece of cotton fabric for back of pillow. Complete pillow as you normally would.

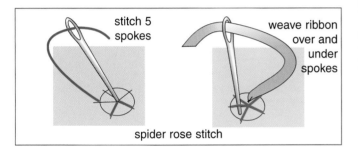

stitch 5 spokes

weave ribbon over and under spokes

spider rose stitch

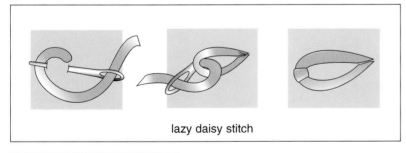

lazy daisy stitch

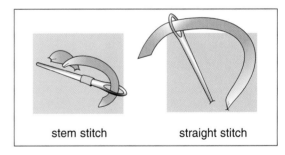

stem stitch · straight stitch

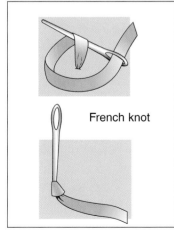

French knot

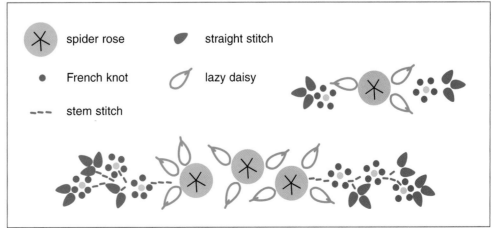

spider rose · straight stitch

French knot · lazy daisy

stem stitch

TISSUE PAPER FRAME

Design by Solange Whitehead for Xyron

SUPPLIES

∾ Frame of choice
∾ Tissue paper of choice (wrinkles look good, so old
  tissue paper will work)
∾ Acid-free glue or Xyron Adhesive Cartridge

INSTRUCTIONS

*Note: Use either acid-free adhesive cartridge or reposition-
able adhesive cartridge, which allows realigning if a pattern is involved.*

1. Wash and dry frame. Cut tissue paper 2" larger than

frame. Cut out center piece, leaving enough to fold
inward and toward back of frame.

2. Glue tissue paper around frame. Separate pieces can
be used for larger frames.

GLOSSARY

ACID FREE

Acid is used in paper manufacturing to break apart the wood fibers and the lignin which holds them together. If acid remains in the materials used for photo albums, the acid can react chemically with photographs and accelerate their detection. Acid-free products have a pH factor of 7 to 8.5. It's imperative that all materials (glue, pens, paper, etc.) used in memory albums or scrapbooks be acid free.

ACID MIGRATION

Acid migration is the transfer of acidity from one item to another through physical contact or acidic vapors. If a newspaper clipping was put into an album, the area it touched would turn yellow or brown. A de-acidification spray can be used on acidic paper or they can be color photocopied onto acid-fee papers.

BUFFERED PAPER

During manufacturing a buffering agent such as calcium carbonate or magnesium bicarbonate can be added to paper to neutralize acid contaminants. Such papers have a pH of 8.5.

CROPPING

Cropping is cutting or trimming a photo to keep only the most important parts.

DIE CUTS

Precut paper shapes used to decorate pages.

JOURNALING

Journaling refers to the text on an album page giving details about the photographs. It can be done in your own handwriting or with adhesive letters, rub-ons, etc. It is one of the most important parts of memory albums because it tells the story behind the photos.

LIGNIN

Lignin is the bonding material that holds wood fibers together as a tree grows. If lignin remains in the final paper product (as with newsprint), it will become yellow and brittle over time. Most paper other than newsprint is lignin free.

MATTING

Background paper used to frame and enhance the photo image.

pH FACTOR

The pH factor refers to the acidity of a paper. The pH scale is the standard for measurement of acidity and alkalinity. It runs from 0 to 14 with each number representing a ten-fold increase. pH neutral is 7. Acid-free products have a pH factor from 7 to 8.5. Special pH tester pens are available to help determine the acidity or alkalinity of products.

PHOTO SAFE

This is a term similar to "archival quality" but more specific to materials used with photographs. Acid-free is the determining factor for a product to be labeled photo safe.

SHEET PROTECTORS

These are made of plastic to slip over a finished album page. They can be side-loading or top-loading and fit 8½″ x 11½″ pages or 12″ x 12″ sheets. It is important that they be acid free. Polypropylene is commonly used. Never use vinyl sheet protectors.

Reprinted from *Making Great Scrapbook Pages,*
Hot Off The Press, Inc.

THE MEMORY EXPERTS

Judy Barker
American
Traditional Stencils

Michele Gerbrandt
Memory Makers

Sandy Cashman
Fiskars, Inc.

Paulette Jarvey
Hot Off The Press

Jennie Dayley
Stickopotamus

Stacy Jullian
Creating Keepsakes

Heidi Geffen
Sticker Planet

Jean Kievlan
Accu-Cut

Deanna Lambson
Creating Keepsakes

Carol Snyder
EK Success

Julie McGuffee
Accu-Cut

Julie Stephani
Krause Publications

Toni Nelson
EK Success

Kate Stephani
Krause Publications

Beth Reames
EK Success

Solange Whitehead
Xyron

Melody Ross
Chatterbox

Photos by Frank Riemer Photography

BEHIND THE SCENES

LEFT: Julie and Michele go over material before taping begins.

RIGHT: Dave said we couldn't tape 16 segments in one day, but we finished by 6:00!

RIGHT: Julie, Ivy Chapman (director), and Dave Larson (producer) look over the daily schedule.

RIGHT: Dale Nicholson helped Carol do a quick ironing touchup between takes.

BELOW: Diane Yokes put the finishing touches on Sandy's makeup.

ABOVE: Melody received candy and flowers for her birthday on the day she was taping.

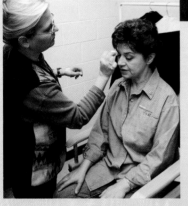

LEFT: Heidi packed up her wardrobe at the end of the day.

RIGHT: Production assistant Sandy Sparks kept everything flowing smoothly in the prep area.